Taste and See

Allergy Relief Cooking

Penny King

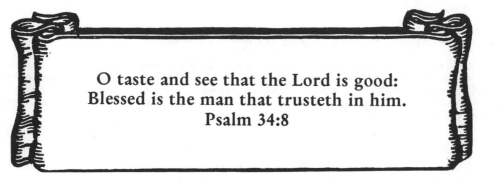

O taste and see that the Lord is good:
Blessed is the man that trusteth in him.
Psalm 34:8

All Scripture quotations are from the King James Version, unless otherwise noted.

Grateful acknowledgment is made for permission to reprint the following recipes and charts:

Tofu Vegetable Quiche, Quick and Easy Tofu Cheesecake, and Corn Chips from Cooking With Natural Foods by Muriel Beltz, Black Hills Health and Education Center, Hermosa, South Dakota 57744,1978.

Tofu Yung and Gravy, Vanilla Tofu Pudding, Zucchini Patties, Ricotta Style Tofu Filling from Tofu Cookery by Louise Haggler, Book Publishing Co. Summertown, Tennessee, 1982.

Bean Thread Oriental Soup and Herb Dressing from Horn of the Moon Cookbook: Recipes from Vermont's Renowned Vegetarian Restaurant, by Ginny Callan, Harper and Row Publishers, 1988.

Soy-Oat Waffles from Oats, Peas, Beans, and Barley Cookbook by Edyth Young Cottrell, Woodbridge Press, Santa Barbara, California 93160,1961.

Sunny Sour Cream, Tofu Rice Loaf, Peach Ice Cream, Carob Peanut Butter Frosting, Banana Popsicle, Date-Nut Bread, Potato Pancake, Lima Bean Chowder, Chickpea A La King, Chicken Style Seasoning, Cashew Pimento Cheese from The Country Life Natural Foods Cookbook, Recipes form the world renowned Country Life Restaurants, Newton, New Jersey.

Tender Rice-Tofu Pancakes, Jack Cheese, Tapioca Fruit Salad from The Joy of Cooking Naturally by Peggy Dameron, Mentone, California 92359,1983.

Nutritional Analysis of Maine Coast Sea Vegetables from Maine Coast Sea Vegetables, Franklin, Maine 04634.

Strawberry Mousse from Nasoya Foods, Leominster, Massachusetts.

Quinoa Tabouli Salad, from Quinoa the Supergrain, by Rebecca Wood, Japan Publications, January 1989.

Ceylonese Rice from Strict Vegetarian by Lorine Tadej.

Nutritional analysis charts for zinc, calcium, iron, and Vitamin C from The New Laurel's Kitchen (c)1986 by Laurel Robertson, Published by Ten Speed Press, Berkeley, California 94707.

Sun Bars, Tahini Oat Cookies, Rice Bread from Uprising: Whole Grain Bakers' Book, C1983 by Uprising Publishing Co.

Millet-Carob.Ice Cream, Slightly Nutty Pudding, Poppy Seed Dressing, Zero Salad Dressing from NEWSTART Homestyle, from Weimar Institute, Weimar California.

NEWSTART (R) is a registered trade mark and is being used with permission from Weimar Institute. A concerted effort has been made to credit the sources of copyrighted materials used in this cookbook. If acknowledgment of a source of any reprint or modification has been overlooked or incorrectly credited, the author will appreciate receiving the information necessary to make appropriate changes or additions.

Contents

Foreword

Certainly Taste and See deserves to be printed and widely distributed. I believe that it will make a real contribution and will fill quite a void in the special diet cookbooks. We see many allergy patients and I would like to have the opportunity of using it in the conditioning center, as well as making it available to other patients with allergies.

I found the chapters on allergies and the immune system very readable and believe that it will be a useful book. The information is scientifically accurate and the author has done a good job of putting such a complex subject into reasonably understandable language.

Several of the Uchee Pines staff members have had an opportunity to look over the manuscript of Taste and See, and the consensus was summed up by one of our staff who said, "If it were available, I would get one right now."

Calvin Thrash Jr. M.D.
President Uchee Pines Institute

Preface

Although some medical scientists and doctors are critical of anecdotal experiences because the proof of effectiveness may not be statistically valid, the editors, in their preface of the American Medical Association publication, The Book of Heart Care, encourage each of us to be "the guardians" of our own health. Preventive medicine is promoted for economy as well as long life. The AMA indicates that they have faith in the American public. They believe that if Americans are given the most current research information in the area of preventive care, the American people will apply this knowledge to their best advantage.

I personally agree with these sentiments, for it is true that our most valuable asset is our health.

Although this cookbook expresses my personal observations of my own experience with food sensitivities, hay fever and eczema, my conclusions are also based on considerable research in the fields of physiology, nutrition and natural healing. While this cookbook has a self-help orientation, it is not meant to replace medical diagnosis or treatment.

With this in mind, I pray this cookbook can be helpful to those who have food-related allergies and to those who have loved ones and friends with allergy problems. If you are not troubled with allergies, you can invite an allergic person to your home to eat. Find out their food sensitivities and use this cookbook to make an appealing and satisfying meal.

Allergy Relief Seminars, with lectures and cooking demonstrations in homes or organizations can be arranged. See last page for address to send for more information.

May God bless you as you seek to learn the best ways to minister to the physical needs of yourself and others.

Acknowledgements

I wish to gratefully acknowledge the contributions and technical assistance of my husband, Robert King; my children, Joshua Wood, Amber and Noah King, for their critical evaluations at the dining room table; and the many cooks who have been so kind to share their recipes.

Grateful acknowledgment goes also to my mother, Marjorie Raymond, and to Jenifer Whitney and Dover Publications for the artistic resources used in illustrating this cookbook.

Special thanks also to the public library staff in New Canaan, Connecticut, and Keene, New Hampshire, and to the staff at Family Health Publications for their help in bringing this book to completion.

Allergy
Know How

The Immune System

The human body is designed with its own built-in defense mechanism- the immune system. The immune system depends upon other body functions for its effectiveness. Just as the armed forces of the United States work together to defend their nation, the body's defense system resists foreign invaders through the united efforts of the circulatory, lymph, endocrine, and nervous systems working in conjunction with the immune system. Their united goal is resistance.

It is a fascinating study to investigate the various components of our body's defense system, ways we can best help these forces to utilize their ammunition, and the problems that can arise from subversion in the ranks. Without our conscious awareness legions of white blood cells are constantly vigilant, guarding our health. We can learn lessons of watchfulness and alertness from these soldier friends. The key is to give the body the best vantage point to resist the enemies that bombard it. Chemicals, toxins, bacteria, and viruses assault us on the highway, in stores, and in other public places which we cannot always avoid. Evasion is an important protective strategy, but it is essential to give our body the upper hand to be able to meet the enemy head on.

We cannot structurally pinpoint the beginning and ending of the immune system as we can with the digestive or reproductive systems. Like the circulatory or nervous system, the immune system is on call throughout the whole body. The white river of the lymphatic system and the red and blue rivers of the circulatory system are the transportation networks of the immune system. The bone marrow is the breeding ground for the white blood cell soldiers. The thymus, lymph nodes and spleen are the barracks. There are two divisions of white blood cells, referred to as phagocytes and lymphocytes. Granulocytes and macrophages are two types within the phagocyte division. The granulocytes could be considered as the marines while their larger comrades, the macrophages, are the specially trained green berets. This first-line defense unit consists of hard working foot soldiers ready to chase and destroy the enemy. A 150-pound adult has approximately 126 billion phagocytes circulating and ready for action. Their job is to be on the alert and ready to do battle and control the spread of the enemy, while the lymphocytes are preparing to reinforce and transport additional ammunition to the combat zone.

After they are made, the lymphocytes migrate from the bone

marrow to the thymus, lymph nodes and spleen. There are several types of lymphocytes including helper T cells, killer T cells, suppressor T cells and B cells. The T cell brigade matures in the thymus where they go through boot camp and are programmed with the amazing ability to recognize possibly a million different kinds of enemies or antigens. Helper T cells travel throughout the body waiting to make contact with the enemy. Their surveillance techniques are so subtle that not until the last twenty years have scientists been able to pinpoint their place in the defense scheme. The phagocytes are very active and aggressive cells. They attack, engulf and digest the enemy. In comparison, the helper T cells - immune messengers - seemingly travel nonchalantly through the lymph and blood channels, touching each molecule they meet and moving on. All molecules have markers on their surface which communicate to the helper T cells whether the molecule is friend or enemy. The antigen's (enemy's) surface marker information is picked up by the helper T cell, activating the T cell onto the nearest lymph node or to the spleen. Here the helper T cell touches B cells and killer T cells which have been passively waiting to be activated. The B cell receives this antigen information and transforms into a plasma cell whose job is to produce antibodies with the potential to find and attach to that specific antigen. Within the antibody is a chemical antitoxin which will neutralize and destroy the enemy.

When the body has an enemy invasion- for example, in the form of a cut, the phagocyte divisions immediately begin their aggressive search-and-destroy tactics. Pus is an outward sign of the immune system at work. Dead bacteria, as well as exhausted and dead white blood cells, give evidence of the skirmish. Scientists report being able to isolate the actions of one granulocyte on one bacterium. The granulocyte corners, engulfs and destroys the bacterium while the bacterium attempts to evade the granulocyte, giving off poisons and attempting counter attacks. Left alone the granulocyte could not sustain, but the antibodies and killer T cells come to the rescue. When the antibodies arrive at the front lines they attach to the enemy and release their antitoxins, neutralizing the enemy and at the same time coating the bacterium with a substance which helps direct the granulocytes to the enemy. The soldiers of the immune system work together, covering for one another and exemplifying guerrilla warfare at its most efficient level.

Another example of this cooperative effort is the two-way communication between helper T cells and macrophages. Helper

T cells arrive at the battlefield and release lymphokines (chemicals) which communicate to the macrophages to remain and keep fighting. The macrophages group together in response to this message and release their own lymphokines which stimulate the T cells to grow. The multiplying T cells in turn attract more macrophage reserves to the combat zone.

After the battle, the majority of the soldiers die off. Suppressor T cells communicate to the other soldiers that the battle is won and it is time to shut down. Memory cells, a special force of T and B cells, remain after the battle to protect the body from a repeat attack. Before a battle with TB, for instance, there may have been one helper T cell in a million programmed to recognize the TB antigen. After the battle, memory T cells will activate B cells and macrophages to produce more antibodies to stand alert on a long- term basis for possible future attack. This is the basis of immunizations.

This second line of defense is further strengthened by natural killer cells. These troops, better known as NK cells, are on constant alert. Although they are not activated by helper T cells, they are influential in the fight against cancer cells. Properdin is a group of nonimmunologic proteins that also back up immune defense maneuvers. No one part of the defense system is self-sufficient, but several lines of defense assure a dense, protective sentry system. The teamwork of the phagocytes and the lymphocytes reflect the masterful touch of God, their Creator. The immune system succeeds because its members and associates are all present and accounted for, and are working in unison.

Although all the soldiers are interrelated, it appears that there are two distinct but parallel defense strategies at work. The T-cells and phagocytes comprise the cellular defense division of the immune system. These interior-directed forces work on viruses and parasites that infect the insides of healthy cells. The humoral defense, or exterior forces, protect against bacteria, fungi and other pathogens (germs) that travel in the bloodstream. B cells, antibodies and complements are the troops of the humoral defense.

Antibodies work by a lock-and-key strategy. The information that the helper T cell gives to the B cell is programmed into the antibody in its shape as well as in its ammunition. The antigen (enemy) is the lock, and the specific antibody created is the key which locks up and disarms the antigen by first physically connecting with the antigen and then by releasing its ammunition to neutralize the antigen poison.

There are five antibody officers in our body's special police force: IgA, IgM, IgG, IgD, and IgE. IgD antibodies have been identified but their function is as yet not understood. IgA, veteran first-line-of-defense personnel, coat the gastrointestinal tract, make up part of the saliva of the mouth and throat, and are secreted in our tears. IgM antibodies are essential to the triggering of the special forces system of complements. There are nine different types of complement proteins circulating in the bloodstream which are produced by liver cells and macrophages. After IgM antibody locks up an antigen, the very presence of this lock and key bond attracts complement one, or C1, to hook onto IgM. In turn, C1 attracts C2 to hook onto it and the process continues until all nine complements are hooked onto the IgM antigen bond. After C9 is attached, the complement canon is completed and ready to detonate. This amazing chemical chain reaction is targeted toward the enemy while the body's own cells are not affected under normal conditions. Scientists are considering that some diseases may result from an upset in the immune system's delicate balance and that lymphocytes turn traitor against the body itself.

IgG antibodies as well as being complement hookups that help fight infection, are smaller than IgM antibodies and are able to cross the placenta from mother to fetus. An amazing display of balance is portrayed as the T and B cells of the mother are targeted to reject the fetus as an enemy antigen, but are repelled by part of the tissue of the placenta, called the trophoblast, which originates from the fetus and protects the fetus from the mother's attacking immune system. The problems many mothers have during the first three months of pregnancy may be related to this counterpoise that transpires between mother and fetus during this crucial attachment process.

In embryo and at birth a baby is dependent on the mother for its immunity. The trophoblast acts as a "selective filter", permitting helpful IgG antibodies to pass from the mother to the fetus via the placenta. Breast feeding plays an essential part in developing the newborn's immune defense system. Antibodies in mother's milk give the baby the protection it needs against disease until it can develop its own supply. Researchers in England have found that breast-fed babies have a six-times lower mortality rate than do bottle-fed infants. Infants who are bottle-fed, or given cereal before their digestive tracts are capable of starch digestion, have a higher incidence of food allergies.

IgE antibodies appear to be working against the body. These IgE subversives bind with an allergen rather than an antigen. An allergen is not a normal body enemy but rather an annoying intruder like dust, pollen or undigested food molecules that an otherwise healthy body can deal with. The bond of IgE and allergen releases histamines (normal internal cell chemicals meant to remain inside the cell except during the necessary inflammation process) rapidly from mast cells. Mast cells are specialized connective tissue cells which aid in blood clotting and play a part in normal inflammatory responses. It is the histamines that cause the hypersensitive reactions of hay fever, anaphylaxis or hives. Recent research has uncovered two lymphokines which T-cells produce. One stimulates the body to produce IgE antibodies, and a second suppresses or stops the production of IgE antibodies. This balance obviously effects the strength or weakness of the body's response to allergens.

Immunologists conclude that heredity can influence a predisposition to allergies because it is known that lymphocytes are programmed as a result of immune response genes. If your parents had asthma or allergies towards cat dander, you may not have those specific allergies, but rather a propensity to allergies in general. Most of the destructive responses of IgE antibodies are a mystery to scientists and physicians. For instance, why is one individual in a family negatively affected by his environment and another is not, or why should one person have an extreme reaction and another a mild reaction and another no reaction to the same antigen?

I believe the allergic person has a major part to play in helping his immune system to positively respond to troublesome allergens. Following the Eight Laws of Health provides the ammunition that the white blood cells need to grow and prosper. Adequate water drinking provides the white and red rivers in our body with a free-flowing transportation channel. Daily showers or baths increase our white blood cell count. Good nutrition keeps the channels open and flowing. High fat, high cholesterol and high sugar diets clog the arteries with sticky blood cells, and accumulated plaque causes traffic jams and detours. Fats lower T cell counts, as do alcohol and tobacco. Just as a garden needs to be fertilized, our thymus, according to Health (January 1985), prospers from a balanced diet. Zinc deficiency is correlated with immunity problems. Whole grains, beans and seaweed are good sources of zinc (refer to zinc source chart).

Exercise in the fresh air and sunshine stimulates the thymus and influences our moods positively. Positive imagery and stress reduction have a significant impact on the immune system. Peace of mind increases the T cells. Researchers know that bereaved spouses are more vulnerable to infections, as are students studying for exams. Our goal should be to help our surveillance and police forces to resist infection by life-style habits that give the white blood cells an overwhelming advantage over the enemies.

Science News (July 29,1982) affirms the connection of enkephalins and endorphins (brain opiate pain killers) with the T cells' fight against cancer. Researchers at the University of Texas Medical School in Galveston report that B and T cells make their own endorphins. At Scripps Clinic in La Jolla, California, beta endorphins have been shown to affect the production of T cells. The body's ability to withstand disease is enhanced as the endocrine and nervous systems join in the fight against infection.

I had a recent experience which tested my body's defense capabilities. I had a tooth extracted which was infected at the root tip. The dentist performed oral surgery and because the tooth was broken he had to cut the gum and use four stitches to close the wound. He insisted on giving me prescriptions for pain relief and antibiotics. I questioned the use of drugs and asked if he was aware of charcoal's ability to fight infection. He conceded that I could be a martyr and forgo the pain medication, but he insisted that I use the antibiotics. He warned me not to use aspirin as it causes bleeding. I did not argue, but as I had been studying about endorphins and the immune system I had more faith in my body's ability to deal with this infection than I had in drugs.

To the best of my knowledge I had been following the Eight Laws of Health. I added various natural remedies to give my defense system the boost it needed for a quick victory over infection. My tooth was extracted after breakfast, so I fasted until the next morning. Fasting the first 12 to 24 hours of sickness will increase the white blood cell count. I drank copious amounts of water and kept a cold ice compress on the area to relieve any swelling. I made a small charcoal poultice and kept it directly on the area for six hours at a time before changing it. I slept quite well that night.

Nutrition is important to the immune system. What you eat and what you refrain from eating can make quite a difference between winning or losing the battle. I avoided all sugars, refined and unrefined. That meant no fruits or fruit juices and, obviously, no honey, barley malt or pure maple syrup. Too much sugar in the blood stream clogs the roadways and depresses white blood cell efficiency. Sugar can be an enemy to white blood cells. Vitamin C and zinc boost the immune system, so I made a special effort to eat foods high in vitamin C but low in sugar, such as collards, red peppers, brussels sprouts, and cabbage. I squeezed one lemon each morning and drank the juice with a glass of water before breakfast. Eating vegetables for my two meals was a blessing, as I found myself with energy in spite of the infection in my mouth. I also drank echniacea root tea and golden seal tea which were recommended by a friend because of their effectiveness to help fight infections.

After 24 hours I used hot and cold to the area. Each evening when I took a shower I directed the spray on my cheek, letting the hot water run for three minutes and then switching to cold for 30 seconds. I repeated this series three times. Special attention to adequate rest and exercise were helpful, as well as time spent in the sunshine each day, even though this occurred in December. All things did work together or good. Full healing took three weeks, but I was then able to resume normal brushing, use of the water pick, and flossing of the area. One of the blessings of this experience was how my peace of mind increased by my active role in the process (please refer to the article entitled Trust in Divine Power-Peace of Mind).

The blessings of participating in the healing process has potent side effects for children, as well. In dealing with earaches and other infirmities contracted by my children, ages 11, 13, and 21, I have found their peace of mind and healing increased by their active role in the simple remedies we used. Following directions for a foot bath, feeling the warmth of a hot water bottle on your ear, holding a poultice in place, or playing with water toys during a hot half-bath, have all resulted in distracting the children from their discomfort as they became occupied with the action taking place. Because most natural remedies take time, it is a choice opportunity to investigate the possible reasons that might have caused the problem. Lead your child to reason from cause to effect so they might desire to make beneficial life-style choices that will help their body to resist further sickness. Time spent during a treatment can be occupied by discussion about the white blood cell soldiers who are courageously fighting the battle and how the child can help their soldiers by not eating excessive amounts of sweets. Take appropriate books from the library illustrating the body systems, and let your children view the inside story of their body setup.

At seven years old, my daughter received a green stick fracture to her right forearm and dislocated her right elbow in a fall. The orthopedic surgeon had to press the fracture to straighten it and pull on her arm to relocate the elbow without the use of any pain medication. Amber felt pain and cried, but this only lasted about one minute, as she felt relief from the bones being reset. If she had been given pain medication, she would not have been able to feel her body recover from the pain, and the side effects of the drugs would have lasted for hours. Some may say that I am a martyr or that I allow my children to experience unnecessary pain through the rejection of the casual use of pain medication and antibiotics; rather, I believe that I am allowing the children the opportunity to see for themselves the great capabilities of the human body's defense system. Yes, our body is a well designed mechanism meant to endure and survive. We have a part to play, and it is a wonderful privilege to study and apply the Eight Laws of Health which are an integral part of the immune system's maintenance and recovery plan.

References:
1. Andewa, Lori B., "Take Good Care of Yourself," *Parents*, July 1984, pp. 43 - 47.
2. Baldwin, Marjorie, MD, "Science Takes a New Look at an Old Remedy," *Life and Health*, January 1974.
3. Barnard, Christian, *The Body Machine*, Crown, New York, 1981.
4. Check, William Ph.D., "Behind Every Healthy Woman," *Health,* January 1985.
5. Cousins, Norman, *Anatomy of an Ilness*, Bantam, 1979.
6. Glasser, Ronald MD, *The Body is the Hero*, Random House, NY, 1976.
7. Lee, Sang, MD, "Allergies," Weimar Tape Ministry, Weimar CA 95736.
8. Maier, Steven, "Stress and Health: Exploring the Links," *Psychology Today*, August 1985, pp. 44 - 49.
9. Marx, Jean L, "The Immune System Belongs in the Body," *Science*, March 8, 1985, pp. 1190 - 1192.
10. Mizel, Stephen and Jaret, Peter, *In Self Defense*, Harcourt Brace, NY, 1985.
11. Nourse, Alan E., MD, *Your Immune System*, Franklin Watts, NY, 1982.
12. *Science News*, "Now Brain Proteins Fight Disease," July 24,1982, p. 55.
13. Tichy, William, *Poisons, Antidotes, and Anecdotes*, Sterting Publishing, NY, 1979, pp. 68-70.
14. Tonegawa, Susumu, "The Molecules of the Immune System," *Scientific American*, October 1985, pp.122-131.
15. Thrash, Agatha, MD, and Thrash, Calvin, MD, *Home Remedies*, New Lifestyle Books, Seale, Alabama, 1981.

Sources of Iron

RDA is 10 - 18mg.

mg.

mg.	Food	Amount
10.5	Prune Juice	1 cup
8.2	Apricots (dried)	1 cup
7.9	Black Beans	1 cup (cooked)
7.8	Walnuts	1 cup
6.9	Garbanzos	1 cup (cooked)
6.7	Almonds	1 cup
6.1	Pinto Beans	1 cup (cooked)
5.1	Lima Beans (dry)	1 cup (cooked)
4.9	Soybeans	1 cup
4.8	Rice bran	1/4 cup
4.4	Rice Polishings	1/4 cup
4.3	Lima Beans (green)	1 cup (cooked)
4.2	Lentils	1 cup (cooked)
4.0	Spinach	1 cup (cooked)
3.9	Peach Halves (dried)	5 halves
3.9	Millet (dry)	1/4 cup
3.7	Parsley	1 cup
3.4	Sunchokes	4 small
3.4	Split Peas (green)	1 cup (cooked)
3.2	Blackstrap Molasses	1 Tablespoon
2.9	Fresh Peas	1 cup
2.8	Beet Greens	1 cup
2.6	Raisins	1/2 cup
2.6	Chard	1 cup
2.4	Dates	10 medium
2.4	Sesame Meal	1/4 cup
2.3	Tofu	4 oz.
2.2	Tomato juice	1 cup
2.1	Wheat Berries (dry)	1/3 cup
2.1	Butternut squash	1 cup (baked)
2.0	Pumpkin Seeds	2 Tablespoons
1.9	Wheat bran	1/4 cup
1.9	Wheat Germ	1/4 cup
1.8	Kale	1 cup
1.8	Prunes	5 (cooked)
1.7	Acorn Squash	1/2 (baked)
1.7	Brussels Sprouts	8 (cooked)
1.5	Collards	1 cup (cooked)
1.5	Strawberries	1 cup
1.4	Potato	1 large (cooked)
1.4	Broccoli	1 stalk
1.4	Oatmeal	1 cup (cooked)

From *The New Laurel's Kitchen*, © 1986, published by Ten Speed Press, Berkeley, CA 94707.

Sources of Vitamin C

Adult RDA is 45 mg.

Fresh Fruits

mg.

mg.		
240	Guava	1 medium
170	Papaya	1 medium
120	Orange Juice	1 cup
90	Cantaloupe	1/2 melon
88	Strawberries	1 cup
81	Mango	1 medium
66	Orange	1 medium
54	Grapefruit	1/2 medium
39	Lemon	1 medium
31	Red Raspberries	1 cup
30	Blackberries	1 cup
27	Tangerine	1 medium
26	Pineapple	1 cup (diced)
20	Blueberries	1 cup
12	Banana	1 medium

Raw Vegetables

150	Red Pepper	1 medium (sweet)
94	Green Pepper	1 medium
42	Cabbage	1 cup (chopped)
28	Tomato	1 medium
28	Spinach	1 cup
20	Mung Bean Sprouts	1 cup

Cooked Vegetables

160	Broccoli	1 stalk
140	Brussels Sprouts	8 sprouts
140	Collard Greens	1 cup
100	Kale	1 cup
71	Kohlrabi	1 cup
70	Green Pepper	1 medium
69	Cauliflowerettes	1 cup
67	Mustard Greens	1 cup
50	Tomato	1 cup
50	Spinach	1 cup
48	Cabbage	1 cup
44	Rutabagas	1 cup
34	Turnip	1 cup
32	Peas	1 cup
32	Okra	1 cup
29	Lima Beans (green	1 cup
28	Chard Leaves	1 cup
25	Sweet Potato	1 boiled
22	Potato	1 boiled

From *The New Laurel's Kitchen*, © 1986, published by Ten Speed Press, Berkeley, CA 94707.

Sources of Zinc

Adult RDA 15mg.

mg.		
5.9	Soy Meal	3.5 oz.
5.7	Wheat Bran	1 cup
3.2	Wheat Germ	1/4 cup
3.1	Rice Bran	1 cup
3.0	Black-eyed Peas	1 cup
2.9	Whole Wheat Flour	1 cup
2.3	Wheat Berries	1/3 cup (dry)
2.1	Cornmeal	1 cup (dry)
2.1	Green Peas	1 cup (cooked)
2.0	Garbanzos	1 cup (cooked)
1.8	Beans, common	1 cup (cooked)
1.4	Soy Flour	1 cup
1.3	Buckwheat whole	1/3 cup (dry)
1.3	Spinach	1 cup (cooked)
1.2	Oatmeal	1 cup (cooked)
1.2	Brown Rice	1 cup (cooked)
1.0	Soy Protein	1/4 cup
0.8	White Flour	1 cup
0.6	White Rice	1 cup

From *The New Laurel's Kitchen*, © 1986, published by Ten Speed Press, Berkeley, CA 94707.

CANKER SORES

The causes of canker sores, or mouth ulcers, are uncertain but could possibly be attributed to viral infections, allergies, stress, vitamin deficiencies, or hormonal imbalance. When I went on an elimination diet, I found most grains to be offenders and consequently gave up eating wheat, rye, rice, barley, and oats, and rotated millet and buckwheat. Canker sores have always been a problem for me, but their numbers and occurrences increased after eliminating grains from my diet. The Annals of Allergy, May 1980 issue, reported that 56% of a group of people examined for food allergies had a history of canker sores. Reasoning from cause to effect, in my case, vitamin deficiencies and an allergic tendency seemed to lower my resistance to mouth ulcers.

Topical application of zinc shows unscientific, but guarded, positive results with my canker sores. Rodale Press' *Complete Book of Minerals for Health* suggests that zinc gluconate tablets, pulverized into a powder and applied to the mouth ulcer, brings healing. Pulverize a tablet by using a teaspoon and a tablespoon as mortar and pestle. Crush the zinc tablet in the tablespoon with the back of the teaspoon. Moisten the tip of a cotton-tipped applicator with the zinc gluconate powder and apply to your sore every 3 to 4 hours. Instead of one to two weeks of aggravation, my canker sores healed in one to three days using the zinc applications.

In the *Southern Medical Journal*, May 1977, a study was reported on seventeen patients with canker sores that responded to zinc supplementation. Twelve improved and had no reoccurrences, or fewer, smaller and less painful sores. These results were similar to Australian studies with cold sores. Canker sores and cold sores respond to similar treatments, but cold sores or fever blisters are caused by a virus - herpes simplex type.[1]

Dr. David Wrary, of the Glasgow Dental Hospital and School in Scotland, believes that people with recurrent episodes of canker sores are iron- as well as zinc-deficient. He has his patients rinse their mouths with zinc chloride or zinc sulfate mouthwash and take zinc and iron supplements.

Dr. Agatha Thrash, in her book *Natural Remedies*, recommends drinking enough water to keep the urine pale, 10-minute hot water gargles, and a moistened goldenseal tea bag applied directly to the sore. Goldenseal has proven successful as a healing agent for me personally. An ice cube held to the sore, when you first sense an ulcer erupting, can stop the sore before it progresses.2

Eliminating alcoholic beverages, chocolate, chewing gum, sharp foods like potato chips, highly seasoned foods, and citrus decreases irritation to the already sensitive sore.

Some researchers conclude that canker sores are an indication of a weak immune system. Both zinc and iron rich foods boost the immune system. Whole grains and beans are excellent sources of zinc. Iron is found in many fruits, nuts, beans, grains, and vegetables (Refer to the enclosed chart on Sources of Iron and Zinc.)

References:
1.Faelten, Sharon, *The Complete Book of Minerals for Healing*, Rodale Press, Emmaus, PA, 1981.
2.Thrash, Agatha, MD, and Thrash, Calvin, MD, *Natural Remedies: A Manual*, Family Health Publications, Sunfield, MI 48890

Learning About Seaweed

Seaweed has been a beneficial food for people around the world who live near oceans. Usually we equate seaweed with the island inhabitants of the Orient, but Scottish, Irish, British, Scandinavians, Russians, and Hawaiians have found seaweed to be a nutritious addition to their diets. The United States, including Hawaii, has 124,000 miles of tidal shore which is quite a potential "wild" sea forest. Seaweed is harvested in Maine, California, Washington, and Florida. The United States imports about six million dollars worth of Nori from Japan each year. Nori is the wrapper used for Japanese style sushi or rice rolls.

You have probably eaten more seaweed than you might think. Algin, a gel-like substance found in brown kelp, and carrageen, the colloid part of Irish moss, are used extensively as thickening agents and binders for such prepared foods as salad dressings, ice creams, puddings, chocolate confections, and baked goods.

For the person with allergies, experimenting with seaweed should be a consideration, as seaweeds are known as sources of trace minerals such as zinc, which plays an important part in the immune system's resistance strategies. Seaweed was once considered a reliable source of vitamin B-12 but recent studies indicate the B-12 is there but is inactive and does not satisfy human nutritional needs. Seaweed also contains calcium, iron and vitamin A. Seaweed is high in sodium, but you can rinse and brush excess salts before using it. The levels vary with each type, so please refer to the composition source chart that follows.

The most familiar seaweed to most is kelp which can be purchased in a convenient powder form and is used as a substitute for salt. I have experimented some with kombu and wakame seaweeds. When you begin cooking split pea soup, add a strip or two of seaweed. After the soup is done, blend it in your blender. Evidence of the seaweed disappears so that those unaccustomed to seaweed won't be offended by the texture of the cooked sea vegetable. A strip of wakame or kombu an be used to make a vegetarian soup stock along with onions, garlic and celery. In a dry skillet, set at low to medium, and toast wakame. As it toasts, the seaweed opens up and the toasted leaves have a salty, potato chip taste and crunch. Lightly toast nori sheets by holding the edges of the sheet with your hands directly above - but not on the top of - an electric or gas burner set at low heat, and eat it long with vegetables, use it as a pocket or scoop for rice, or crumple and sprinkle on top of soup. Any toasted or ground seaweed is good added to sesame gamazio instead of salt. Refer to the index for other seaweed recipes.

Agar-agar is a family favorite because of its gelling ability, as is Emes vegetable gelatin which has carrageen as its base. You can use these two seaweeds to make firm "Jell-O's" or soft custards. Recipes can be found under Sugarless Desserts.

Arame, hijiki and dulse are other seaweeds that are available in natural food stores. Check into macrobiotic or oriental cookbooks for recipes using these seaweeds. I plan to continue experimenting with seaweeds and introducing them to my family. The adventure of experimenting with unfamiliar foods can be exciting and challenging, while seaweed offers new tastes and a variety of textures to add your dietary repertoire.

References:

1. Crane, Milton G., "Vitamin B-12 in Total Vegetarians," *Health and Healing*, Vol. 10, No. 4, pp. 4 - 5.
2. Kushi, Michio, *The Book of Macrobiotics*, Japan Publishing, 1977, p.178.
3. Madlener, Judith Cooper, *The Sea Vegetable Book*, Clarkson N. Potter, NY, 1977.
4. Marx, Wesley, "Seaweed, The Ocean's Unsung Gilt'," *Reader's Digest*, June 1984, pp. 39 - 48.
5. Wollner, David, "Shoppers Guide to Natural Foods," *East West Journal*, Sept. 1981, pp. 38 - 42.
6. "News Digest," *Vegetarian Times,* September, 1991, pp 24, 25.

NUTRITIONAL ANALYSIS OF MAINE COAST SEA VEGETABLES

	PROTEIN g/100gms	FAT g/100gms	CARBOHYDRATE g/100g	CALORIES cal./100g	CALCIUM mg/100g (C)	POTASSIUM mg/100g (K)	MAGNESIUM mg/100g (Mg)	PHOSPHOROUS mg/100g (P)	IRON mg/100g (Fe)	SODIUM mg/100g (Na)	IODINE mg/100g (I)	MANGANESE mg/100g (Mn)	COPPER mg/100gms (Cu)	CHROMIUM mg/100gms (Cr)	FLUORIDE mg/100gms (F)	ZINC mg/100gms (Zn)	VIT A I.U. (V-A)	VIT B₁ (Thiamine) mg/100gms (V-B₁)	VIT B₂ (Riboflavin) mg/100gms (V-B₂)	VIT B₃ (Niacin) mg/100gms (V-B₃)	VIT B₆ (Pyrodoxine) mg/100gms (V-B₆)	VIT B₁₂ (Cyanocobalamin) mcg/100gms (V-B₁₂)	VIT C mg/100g (V-C)	VIT E I.U. (V-E)
ALARIA	17.7	3.6	39.8	262	1100	7460	918	503	18.1	4240	16.6	1.02	.172	210	4.3	3.44	8487	.558	2.73	10.5	6.23	5.03	5.90	4.92
DULSE	21.5	1.7	44.6	264	213	7820	271	408	33.1	1740	5.20	1.14	.376	150	5.3	2.86	663	.073	1.91	1.89	8.99	6.60	6.34	1.71
KELP	16.1	2.4	39.3	241	942	11200	900	423	42.6	4460	144	1.23	.148	240	3.9	2.86	561	.549	2.48	3.62	8.63	2.60	4.16	2.71
NORI	28.4	4.5	45.1	318	188	2680	378	408	20.9	1610	1.40	3.46	.612	120	5.8	4.15	4286	.577	2.93	5.92	11.21	17.5	12.03	5.09
RDA	57g*	77g*	345g	2300 cal.*	800mgs†	1875-5625mgs††	350mgs†	800mgs†	10mgs†	1100-3300mgs††	.15mgs†	2.5-5mgs††	2-3mgs††	.05-.20mgs††	1.5-4.0mgs††	15mgs†	5000 I.U.†	1.4mgs†	1.6mgs†	18mgs†	2.2mgs†	3mcg†	60mgs†	15 I.U.†

MACRONUTRIENTS · **MAJOR MINERALS** · **TRACE MINERALS** · **MAJOR VITAMINS**

Please remember that all the statistics in this chart have only relative significance. The whole plants provide much more than the sum of their parts.

*These macronutrient guidelines are determined by assuming that an adult male's recommended daily energy intake of 2300 calories is derived from 10% protein, 30% fat, and 60% carbohydrate, according to the U.S. Dietary Guidelines.
†Recommended Dietary Daily Allowances, or RDA's are determined by the National Academy of Sciences as nutritional guidelines for "good" health for "most" people in the U.S.A.

††Ranges of recommended daily intake are provided by the Academy where there is insufficient information on which to determine an exact RDA. Figures in both categories are for a middle aged, middle weight, American male.
These nutritional assays were done by Silliker Laboratories of New Jersey and the Plant and Soil Analytical Lab., University of Maine at Orono.

g/100gms, grams per 100 grams.
100 grams = 3.5 ounces
mg/100gms, milligrams per 100 grams
I.U., International Units or mg/100gms
mcg., micrograms

Maintaining Good Health

What is health? *The American College Dictionary* defines health as freedom from disease, vigor and soundness of body. The opposite of health is "sick." The American public is supporting spas, weight control clinics, hospitals, doctors, vitamin companies, and health food stores, as they spend millions seeking health.

You don't need to pay anyone to achieve health. Health is a matter of personal responsibility and most people can attain soundness of body by following simple, healthful principles, and all it will cost you is thought, decision and time.

You can have a **NEWSTART**® by committing yourself each day to health. Following is a daily checklist. Follow each step day by day and you will soon find yourself free from fatigue, boredom and depression. If you are already healthy, these principles can help you to stay healthy. Each letter in **NEWSTART**® is a reminder of one of the eight laws of health.

Nutrition: Eat well of whole grains, fruits and vegetables. Eat less of refined sugars, fats and processed foods. The National Academy of Sciences says 30% to 40% of cancer is believed to have a direct connection to diet. Diet can not only keep your disposition happy and your complexion bright, but it can also keep your allergy under control and lessen your risk of coronary heart disease, high blood pressure and cancer.

Exercise in the open air at least three times a week. Walking and gardening are good moderate exercises.

Water: Drink 6 - 8 glasses of water daily. Abraham Lincoln toasted his presidential victory with a glass of water because he believed water to be the best beverage.

Sunshine: Soak in the sunshine at least 15 minutes each day to collect your daily quotient of vitamin D.

Temperance: Abstain from all those things that can hurt you, such as alcohol, nicotine and caffeine, and use moderately those things which are good. Even too much of a good thing can be harmful.

Air: Fresh air is more important to people than food and drink. While exercising, breath deeply so your lungs, brain and blood vessels can be refreshed.

Rest: Learning to relax and getting adequate sleep can help your body respond positively to negative stress.

Trust in Divine Power: Be thankful for your blessings and seek to help others.

Each day you can have a **NEWSTART**® as you become involved in your own health and take responsibility for putting these principles into practice. Think health. Decide health. You can achieve health!

Nutrition

Picture a dart board and instead of points put your sights on top nutrition. Think of the bull's-eye filled with foods which give you a powerhouse of nutrition but are low in fat and refined sugars, and balanced with full - rather than empty - calories.

In the center you want to aim for unprocessed foods like broccoli, and other dark leafy greens such as kale. Whole grains would include brown rice and millet, beans such as garbanzos and lentils, and vegetables such as white and sweet potatoes, cauliflower, winter squash, garlic, and carrots. Include fresh fruits such as bananas, melons, apples, oranges, and seeds and nuts such as almonds, sunflower seeds, and home-grown alfalfa sprouts. All these super foods are famous for their immune enhancing capabilities.

Keep your sights on the bull's-eye and every day attempt to include these whole grains, fruits, vegetables, legumes, nuts, and seeds in your diet. Simplicity at each meal, with a wide variety over your week's menu, will guarantee proper nutrition.

On the next ring of- the target are foods that are good but just not so nutrition- packed. You can choose from corn, tomatoes, oatmeal, pineapple, pears, fresh berries, squash, beets, parsley, green peppers, onions, carob, sesame seeds, and tahini.

The next ring would include processed or concentrated foods such as whole grain breads, tofu, pastas, peanut butter, dried fruits like raisins and dates, avocados, granola, and unsweetened juices.

The outer ring consists of foods to use occasionally and in small quantities. Dairy products, canned fruits and vegetables, honey, molasses, coconut, oil, and prepared spreads.

There are some foods which should be avoided and are not on the target area. Avoid caffeine drinks such as coffee, tea and soda. Avoid also alcohol, chocolate, sugar-dominated candy and breakfast cereals, refined-grain baked goods, pickles, hot-dogs, bacon, and deep-fried snack foods.

A more detailed description of the Nutrition Bull's-Eye can be found in a Rodale Press publication, *Home Food Systems*, edited by Roger Yepsn. Your diet will be right on target the closer you come to eating the foods in the bull's-eye. Change is not always easy, but when we have a good reason to change, and have alternatives with which to make the changes, it becomes easier. Good health can be achieved through careful choices. Seek for the best. *Something Better* is the challenge. Act on good health today.

Exercise

Fresh air is more important to our health than the food we eat or the water we drink. It would be to our advantage to re-evaluate the time spent in the fresh air. Studies have shown that men who smoke, yet exercise on a regular basis, have less sickness than sedentary nonsmokers who do no regular exercise. I am not condoning smoking; rather I am promoting regular, moderate exercise. Not only do physically active people have less sickness, but when they do get sick they bounce back to health faster than inactive people. Exercise gives all the body systems the capability to resist disease.

Your choice of exercise is a personal matter, taking into consideration your age, weight and preferences. Whole-body exercise in the open air is best. Exercising moderately fifteen to 30 minutes without interruption, to work up a sweat and get your heart pumping beyond your normal rhythm, is essential. Three times a week is adequate. Remember: *brisk sustained and regular* are the keynotes to developing a profitable exercise program.

Exercise is life-giving. Exercise strengthens the muscles. Your heart is a muscle that needs to be exercised beyond your normal routine activities. Exercise helps your brain to think clearly. Exercise helps the stomach digest food, and it increases the circulation of blood throughout the whole body. Efficient blood circulation keeps one healthy and composed. Exercise burns more calories and consequently depresses your appetite. Exercise makes your cheeks rosy - a natural makeup.

Exercise in the open air. Exercise by walking or working in the garden. Exercise your arms. Exercise your legs. Exercise by helping someone. Exercise your smile. Exercise is one of nature's doctors. Plan out a moderate exercise program and stick to it. Your heart, your brain, your lungs, your muscles, your whole body, will appreciate your decision. Health is preserved by exercise. Make exercise a habit.

Water

Approximately 70% of the human body is water. Water is the main ingredient in human blood. The fluids inside and around our body cells are made up of water. Water is part of the body's transportation system as it carries dissolved nutrients throughout the body and flushes wastes out. Water regulates the body temperature. We lose between 2 and 3 quarts of water each day as sweat, moisture in our breath, and through waste. A basketball player may lose as much as 15 pints of water during a game. This lost water must be replaced.

Thirst is not an appropriate indicator of our water need. Take your body weight and divide it by 2 and divide that number by 8 to determine how many glasses of water you need to drink each day.

Water has been replaced as a main drink by coffee, tea, sodas, juices, milk, and alcohol. The majority of the volume of these beverages is water, but along with the water comes caffeine, added calories, sugar, fat, and brain cell suffocation caused by alcohol-soaked, sticky red blood cells.

Economics is also a factor. Water is basically a free or low cost beverage. Timing is also a factor in water drinking. Our stomachs become a lake when we drink during our meals. Excess liquid dilutes the digestive juices and slows down digestion. The best between-meal snack is water. Drink 1 - 2 glasses of warm water first thing when you get up in the morning. Drink a glass or two at midmorning and a half hour before you eat. Finish up your quota by drinking several glasses in the afternoon. Often times you think you are hungry because your stomach grumbles, yet a glass of water will satisfy.

The allergic person should pay careful attention to water drinking because many chemical reactions of the body depend upon the presence of ample water. A defective immune system is the basic cause of all allergies. It makes sense to give your interrelated body systems the best advantage possible. Giving the body ample water inside and out, regular exercise in the fresh air and sunshine, moderate yet sufficient amounts of whole foods, adequate rest, and peace of mind, can give that needed boost to the immune system. Make water drinking a habit. Consider quantity and timing, and give your body the lift it needs.

References
1. Berger, Melvin, *The New Water Book,* Thomas Crowell, NY, 1973.
2. Johnson, G. Timothy, *The Harvard Medical School Health Letter Book,* Cambridge, MA, 1981.

Sunshine

A well-functioning body requires daily exposure to sunlight or ultraviolet light. Benefits from sunshine are derived from spending a minimum of 30 to 60 minutes per day out doors. Exposure to ultraviolet light lowers blood pressure, lowers cholesterol, lowers blood sugar, increases glycogen in the liver, increases adrenaline in tissues, increases tolerance to stress, increases the body's resistance to infection, boosts the immune system by increasing the white blood cell count, and increases the skin's resistance towards infection.

Sunlight and sugar metabolism have a significant connection. The absorption of glucose (simple sugar) into the cells is facilitated by sunlight. Sunlight stimulates the body to convert glucose into glycogen (the storage form of glucose in liver and muscles). Sunlight is a stabilizer of blood sugar levels much like insulin, as it reconverts glucose into energy and is instrumental in cell absorption of glucose.[1] This is significant for persons with yeast infections. Excess sugar in the bloodstream depresses the ability of white blood cells to engulf and eliminate unfriendly germs. Candida albicans (normal yeast organisms found in the mucous membranes, especially the intestines and digestive tract) feeds on sugar, causing overproduction of yeast. With a weakened immune system unable to keep the overgrowth under control, allergic responses such as fatigue, stuffy nose, skin problems, vaginitis, and depression, are triggered. As the body is able to metabolize glucose more efficiently with the aid of sunshine and proper diet, there can be better control of the candida albicans. Sugar metabolism is just one aspect of yeast allergies.[2] Further discussion can be found under the heading Yeast Infections elsewhere in this book.

Excess free fats in the diet, and sunbathing, directly contradict each other. Too much free fat in the bloodstream causes a clogging effect and limits the ability of the tissues to utilize oxygen in the bloodstream by 60% to 70%. Experiments performed with mice, which were fed high fat diets and exposed to direct sunlight, revealed that skin cancer is easily provoked. However, when mice were fed low fat diets and then exposed to direct sunlight, the occurrence of skin cancers was minimal.[3] Being judicious in your use of dietary fats makes more sense than staying out of the sunshine for fear of skin cancer.

Sunlight is especially significant to persons with allergies because sunlight boosts the immune system by increasing the number of white blood cells. Sunlight promotes health and healing within our bodies by increasing the white blood cells' ability to destroy bacteria. In some research the ability to engulf bacteria was doubled after exposure to sunlight.[4] Heliotherapy (sunlight therapy) aids in the fight to control infections. In Russia, ultraviolet light therapy is used for miners and school children during winter months because they have found this therapy to cut the number of colds in miners by 50% and shown effectiveness in controlling dental cavities in school children.[5]

The body manufactures vitamin D by absorbing energy from the sun. Cholesterol in the skin is converted into vitamin D when the skin is in contact with sunshine. There is a double blessing here. One, the lowering of cholesterol levels, and two, the production of vitamin D just from spending time in the sunshine. Also, vitamin D is necessary for calcium absorption. Just five minutes with your face exposed to sunlight will supply sufficient vitamin D for the day.[6] Many scientists today are questioning the practice of supplementing foods with vitamin D. Some contend that Americans consume six times the necessary Vitamin D. Milk, cereals, margarine, noodles, and flour are often supplemented with vitamin D.[7]

Researchers found that in the wintertime, elderly residents at the Chelsea Soldier Home near Boston absorbed less calcium from their diets. Richard Wurtman, the director of the neuroendocrine laboratory at the Massachusetts Institute of Technology, and Robert Neer, a medical researcher, increased the calcium absorption of these elderly men by 15% by exposing them to 8 hours of special fluorescent lamps which simulated natural light. Others living at the Home under ordinary incandescent and fluorescent lamps lost 25% of their ability to absorb calcium.[8]

Photobiologists - scientists who study how light interacts with life, explain that indoor lighting lacks the intensity and completeness of sunlight. The spectrum colors found in sunlight of violet, blue, green, yellow, orange, and red cast a full rainbow of light. Incandescent light is mostly yellow, orange and red. Fluorescent light has a wider spectrum of color than incandescent, but is still lacking the fullness of sunlight.[9] The benefit of full spectrum light for the eyes is important for hormonal balance and healing in such diseases as osteoarthritis. Spend time in the sunlight without eyeglasses or contact lenses to glean the full benefit of sunlight.10

Sunlight eliminates bacteria from air, water and skin. Allow the sunlight to penetrate into all the corners of your home. Open up the windows, pull back the curtains, and enjoy the antiseptic effects of the sun and fresh air. Exercise and work in the sunshine daily. Time in the sunshine can be tranquilizing and influences our attitudes in a positive manner. For specific health problems, such as a stuffy nose, eczema or skin ulcers, take 10 to 20 minute sunbathes. After a therapeutic sunbathe, shower or bathe to wash off the perspiration which is a vehicle of the body to expel toxic wastes.11

"Pure air, sunlight, abstemiousness, rest, exercise, proper diet, the use of water, trust in Divine Power -these are the true remedies. Every person should have a knowledge of nature's remedial agencies and how to apply them.

"Nature's process of healing and up-building is gradual, and to the impatient it seems slow. But in the end it will be found that nature, untrammeled, does her work wisely and well. Those who persevere in obedience to her laws will reap the reward of health of body and health of mind."12

Footnote References:
1. "Sunlight: Power to Heal", *Island Terrace Centre: Special Edition*, Middleboro, MA, 1981, p. 4.
2. Crook, William G., MD, *The Yeast Connection*, Professional Books, Jackson, TN, 1983, pp. 9 - 14.
3. "Sunshine," *Newstart® Homestyle*, Weimar Institute, Box 486, Weimar CA, 95736, Section 8, pg.5.
4. Kime, Zane R. MD, MS, *Sunlight Can Save Your Life*, World Health Publications, Penryn, CA, pp. 172,174-178.
5. Hoffman, Jay, PhD, *The Missing Link*, Professional Press Publishing, Valley Center, CA, 1981, pp.317-322.
6. *Newstart® Homestyle*, Section 8, pg. 5.
7. "The Original Vitamin D Machine", *Bodywise*, Concerned Communications, Box 1000, Arroyo Grande, CA, 93420, Vol. 8, #4, pp. 6 - 7.
8. Ponte, Lowell, "How Artificial Light Affects Your Health", *Reader's Digest*, Feb. 1981, pp. 131 - 134.
9. Ibid.
10. *Newstart® Homestyle*, video tape lectures.
11. Hoffman, pp. 366, 376, 388.
12. White, Ellen G., *The Ministry of Healing*, Pacific Press, Mountain View, CA, 1905, p. 275.

Temperance

A car without brakes is as useless as a car without proper acceleration. The human body is much the same. We need a balance of action and inaction. Self-control becomes a guiding principle of life as we learn to understand and to practice the Eight Laws of Health.

Avoiding anything that is harmful will benefit health. Cigarettes, alcohol, drugs, overeating, high fat, high sugar, and highly refined foods are each destructive to the human body. Our goal can be to only partake of that which builds up rather than that which tears down.

Self-control also involves using moderately those things which are good. Too much of a good thing can cause problems. Sunlight heals, but too much sunlight burns and destroys. Wheat, eggs and dairy products are leading allergens in the United States because of overuse and the exclusion of other available and nutritious foods.

When we are burdened with annoying allergy symptoms, it is a blessing to find positive, reasonable and safe alternatives to otherwise problem foods, clothing, cleaning materials, and even thought patterns. To help yourself and others to be willing to make healthful life-style changes, you can begin by offering attractive alternatives. It is my prayer that the recipes in this cookbook can offer examples of something better.

When we are sick we sometimes feel forsaken. The "why me" syndrome plagues us. Disease most often comes because of a distinct reason. Seek out the cause behind your problems. Investigate all avenues. God has blessed man with tremendous thought capabilities to reason out problems. Reasoning from cause to effect, setting realistic goals and learning to make appropriate choices will enable one to work out and stick to elimination and other special diets. It is important to take the time to question ourselves, investigate our past, and connect experiences to conclude what it is in our lives and choices that has led to our symptoms. (Please refer to the Case History Forms.)

I appreciate the balance and discipline set forth in the twelve steps of Alcoholics Anonymous. The goal is self-control, abstinence from alcohol. The path is begun by recognition that the person involved is helpless to change without belief in a Higher Power than himself. The support of the nightly meetings, and a fellow alcoholic sponsor, give the recovering alcoholic added encouragement to face each day - one at a time. The results are impressive, with thousands finding freedom from alcohol addiction. Self-knowledge opens the door to self-improvement. Spiritual support gives one the strength to strive for a seemingly impossible goal. Practicing the discipline of self-control encourages the habit of making the right choices. Repeated success on a daily basis gives the recovering alcoholic the motivation and self-esteem to endure. I find these basic principles to be practical and workable when applied to the challenge of recovering from allergy problems.

Regularity and scheduling enhances and increases our accomplishments. Time management is a positive step toward organizing one's life. I find it helpful to organize appointments, addresses, telephone numbers, birthdays, important dates, and financial information - all in a 6 by 9 loose-leaf notebook small enough to fit in my purse. DAYTIMERS, of Allentown, Pennsylvania, 18001, is a company that sells materials which help us with time management. Service to others is a natural byproduct of practicing self-control. As we bring our own lives into control we have more time and energy to employ in helping others. Time is a precious gift to be shared. Set aside time to read to loved ones or listen to their experiences. Set aside time to take your children or friends to a natural setting and enjoy the health-giving atmosphere of garden, forest, mountain, or ocean. Offer yourself and loved ones the calming stimulus of natural beauty.

Self-control involves what we look at, hear and touch, as well as what we eat. Learning to discriminate between best, mediocre and worst is a skill to be fostered. Differentiating between our needs and our wants gives us perspective as to the value of things and is a step toward simplicity. Being allergic to dust, mold spores and mildew has helped me to simplify. My goal is to own only that which is necessary, rather than to be burdened with excess dust-catching extras. Philippians 4:8 gives us a guideline for excellence:

"Whatsoever things are *true*, whatsoever things are *honest,* whatsoever things are *just*, whatsoever things are *pure,* whatsoever things are *lovely*, whatsoever things are of *good report*; if there be any *virtue*, and if there be any *praise*, think on these things.

Air

The basic needs for survival are air, water, food and shelter. Air is the most important! We all know that without air our life expectancy is limited. Just as air is critical to survival, so it is critical to maintaining good health. Like a car, the human body needs regular tuneups, lubrication and adjustments. Every day we need fresh air, for moment by moment we are changing the air inside our body to refresh our blood and internal organs.

We should look at air as part of our daily sustenance, just as we consider the food we eat. Air is the food for our lungs. Deep breathing encourages good circulation to the upper respiratory passages. Start a new habit of deep breathing. Stand up straight. Put one hand on your lowest rib and your other hand on your stomach. In between is your diaphragm. This is where the action should be when you breathe. Practice abdominal breathing and soon it will become second nature. Normal breathing exchanges 6 quarts of air, while deep breathing exchanges 13 plus quarts of air.

The blood is purified by fresh air. Fresh air is invigorating and helps our vital organs resist disease. We benefit from listening to the mellow breezes of the air. A sense of restfulness and refreshment is brought by the relaxing sound of the air. As with anything in the extreme, over heated air or poorly ventilated rooms can be unhealthy. Impure air is poison. Smoke and dust in the air endangers our health. So be good to your lungs; even in the cold weather get out and breathe in the fresh air. Add sunshine and exercise and you will be benefited with increased energy and vitality.

If you are annoyed by

headaches or stuffy nose, you will profit from regular outdoor deep breathing and exercise. How you choose to exercise each day is an individual decision. Walking is a moderate exercise that can be enjoyed by most. Start out slowly, but increase your distance and briskness so you can work up to a 1/2 to 1 hour walk at a brisk pace. Your heart and lungs will appreciate the effort.

To the person with allergies, fresh air is doubly as important. I always wondered why my allergies abated in the summertime. Now I understand that smoke from wood fires releases mold spores into the air, gas pilot lights emit fumes, and dirty humidifier trays results in mold spores being circulated. Dirty air-conditioning filters can also be responsible for poor quality inside air. It is important to avail yourself of fresh air in the cold months as well as in the warmer months.

Increased indoor air pollution has resulted from better insulation for our homes. Doors and windows are sealed against air leaks more securely, but this can be detrimental to the allergic person. Your lungs need continual airing out, so you must provide good air for the process. Keep your rooms well ventilated. Be a window opener.

Air out your bed sheets each morning by throwing back the covers and exposing them to as much fresh air as possible. Our bodies can perspire as much as 2 cups of water each night, which is absorbed by our sheets and bed clothes. Open up your windows and breathe deeply for a better disposition and general well-being.

They that wait upon the Lord shall renew their strength; they shall mount up with wings as eagles; they shall run and not be weary; and they shall walk and not faint. Isaiah 40:31

Rest

Rest is defined as sleep, relaxation and recreation. Rest is a universal principle. Crops are rotated to avoid soil exhaustion. Apple trees rest over the winter months. Some animals hibernate. Our hearts rest at the end of each beat. Our stomach needs rest after each meal digested. God rested from His work of creating this world, and blessed the seventh day, as a day of special rest for man. These regular patterns of the balance of rest and activity are an encouragement to copy.

Rest comes in different packages. Momentary, daily, weekly, and vacation size rests are all important. We need periodic breaks during the day. Traditional coffee breaks can cause more fatigue than rest if you use caffeine drinks and high fat, high sugar snacks. As stimulants, caffeine drinks - such as coffee, black tea, and colas, excite the brain to activity, but in the same degree that they elevate, they will exhaust. Caffeine drinks are not nourishing to the body system, but create an unnatural nervous excitement. Heavy users often develop tolerance, which then means they must drink even higher doses to obtain the desired effects. Tired nerves need rest and quiet time to recuperate.

Alternatives to food and drink-centered breaks could be a brisk walk in the fresh air and sunshine, indoor exercise, deep breathing, relaxation exercises, a water- drinking break, a time of quiet meditation or reading. For the sedentary office worker, physical exercise would be a restful change from sitting, while the laborer might stretch out and relax to gain rest.

Adequate exercise during the day will better prepare you for sleep at night. A firm bed, regular rising and sleeping times, quietness, darkness, an empty stomach, fresh air from opened windows, and warm feet, are all sleep inducers. A neutral to warm bath and catnip tea can help you when sleeping becomes a problem, but herb teas should not be used as a daily sleep enhancer, as the goal is to learn to sleep without any inducements. Unresolved psychological problems can be sleep blockers. Try to count your blessings rather than tossing and turning. Excessive stimulation from TV programs, eating just before going to bed, or eating in bed, will interfere with deep, restful sleep. Use of caffeine beverages cause insomnia, as do the side effects of alcohol. Check the state of your jaw and teeth. Teeth-grinding and jaw-clenching tend to make sleep difficult. Tensing and relaxing muscles can help relax the body.

We sleep away one-third of our lives. A few can get by with

four hours of sleep and a few need twelve hours, but the average sleep requirement is between seven and nine hours. Large quantities of growth hormones are produced during deep sleep before the hours of midnight. The hormones are essential in repairing and replacing damaged tissue and cells. Healing speeds up during sleep. In order to glean the most from sleep, it makes sense to be aware of the things that help us sleep and those that hinder our sleep.

The Bible, in Genesis 2:2-3 and Exodus 20:8, prescribes a twenty-four-hour day of rest each week, the Sabbath day. The Sabbath allows for a regular and specific time set aside to remind man of the Creator's continuing role in sustaining this world. Time set apart each week to spend with God strengthens the relationship between God and man. The Sabbath is an opportunity to be with family and friends as well as a time to be of service to others. God, in His wisdom, knew that we would need a specific time to recharge our spiritual reserves as well as our physical and mental stores. Also, devotional time each day with yourself and family is important for peace of mind and rest.

Vacations can give one a change from the otherwise hustle and bustle of life in the twentieth century. Stress, tension, pressures, and deadlines put a strain on our storehouse of mental, spiritual and physical cache. Stress, in the form of negative thoughts, anger, jealousy, guilt, and resentment often go right along with us on vacation. Stress is an ingredient of life. How we deal with stress is a key to health. Learning how to rest, relax and sleep during the day, night, week, or month will aid in our achieving optimum well-being. We can tune in and listen to our body's messages of tiredness and exhaustion. The dividends of regular periods of rest are healing, greater productivity, a calm disposition, and more thoughtful reactions towards others.

References:
1.Johnson, Timothy G., MD, *The Harvard Medical School Health Letter Book*, Harvard University Press, Cambridge, MA, 1981, pp. 103 - 108.
2.Ruben, David, MD, *All You Wanted to Know About Nutrition*, Avon, NY, 1979.
3.Video Lecture on "Rest," *Newstart® Homestyle*, Weimar Institute, Box 486, Weimar, CA, 95736.
4.Ward, Brian R., *Body Maintenance*, Franklin Watts, NY, 1983, pp. 42 - 43.

MAINTAINING GOOD HEALTH

Trust in Divine Power

Pain and stress are part of everyone's daily experience; but the allergic person is often more sensitive to his environment, and reactions can range from baffling annoyances to acute medical and emotional problems. The human body has been designed to resist disease and to deal with large amounts of pain. There is an intimate partnership between the body and the mind during the healing process, as well as when the body works

to maintain health. Through the same type of close relationship, God will work with the human mind to bring about security and peace of mind despite extraneous circumstances. Peace of mind plays a major role in the healing process as a link in the chain of the body's defense system.

The Bible recognizes the recuperative powers of thankfulness, gratitude, cheerfulness, singing, hospitality and peace of mind as healing agents. "A merry heart doeth good like a medicine" (Proverbs 17:22) is an example of Biblical psychology. Experts in the fields of medicine and psychology confirm the healing power found in faith and hope. Three different research projects during the 1960's and 1970's resulted in the realization that the body is equipped with a special chemical-control system, the purpose of which is to deal with pain and stress. The facts behind these research projects are fascinating, but space does not allow for detailed descriptions. If you are interested, I encourage you to read the accounts of these studies from the references noted at the end of this article.

The discovery of brain chemicals, called endorphins and enkephalins, has not only affirmed the remedial-centered principles of Christianity, but has opened the way for chemically-centered cures for drug addiction, mental illness, weight management, and chronic pain control. Endorphins and enkephalins are manufactured automatically by many brain centers, as well as the pituitary gland. The pituitary is the smallest gland in our endocrine system, but it is responsible for controlling the on and off switches of most of the other glands. The pituitary is about one-half an inch in diameter, about the size of a marble. Working with the hypothalamus, the pituitary produces and stores hormones which influence growth, reproduction, child birth, breast feeding, and excretion. The pituitary is a marvelous example of the power and influence of little things.

Endorphin is a combination of Greek words meaning "the morphine within." *Enkephalin* means "in the head." These neurochemicals are peptides, or short proteins, made up of amino acids linked together like beads on a chain. Scientists believe there are unknown numbers at work waiting to be detected and defined. Beta-endorphins are classified into two groups, alpha and gamma. Alpha-endorphins, differing from gamma by only one amino acid, tranquilize or stop pain like enkephalins. Gamma endorphins produce the opposite reactions of irritability, violence, and supersensitivity to pain. Etorphine, one type of endorphin, is ten thousand times as powerful as morphine. Endorphins are found in the amniotic fluid which is the liquid that surrounds the baby growing in the mother's uterus. It is speculated that a mother's endorphin production is increased when labor begins. There are endorphins that elicit feelings of hunger or satiation as well as euphoria. Endorphins are opiate-like compounds which, when extracted from man or animals, are highly addictive, just as morphine and heroin. Scientists are attempting to synthesize chemicals to replace habit-forming opiates, diet pills or tranquilizers.

Scientists can measure endorphin levels in the blood. There is a base-line level researchers work with, and they have found that alcoholics and drug addicts have low levels of endorphins. When gamblers gamble, endorphin levels increase. Depression patients given electric shock treatments to the temples show increased endorphin levels. Experimental rats under shock stimulus reveal higher levels of endorphins than before the shock. Self-inflicted mental stress, such as negative thoughts, uncontrolled grief and depression, depreciate endorphin levels. A stressful experience, such as a car or sports related accident, will increase endorphins.

Scientists are experimenting daily to uncover more of the secrets of endorphins and their influences. Yet even our limited knowledge of the functions and influences of endorphins are useful in our quest for peace of mind. The best possible tranquilizers, according to Arthur Janov, psychologist and author of *The Primal Scream*, are our ideas. Ideas tranquilize by setting off the mechanism that will eventually result in the production of endorphins. "To hear praise is not only music to the ears but chemicals to the brain," according to Janov. The influence of hope, faith, praise, singing, thankfulness and laying on of hands to the sick are foundation principles of Christianity as well.

Brainwashing techniques are used to deliberately lower the pain threshold or endorphin levels. The victim is made vulnerable and weak by reducing their physical, emotional and spiritual defenses through torture and deprivation. Then they are offered a way to end the suffering if they reveal whatever it is their captors seek. Whether a person is a hero or a coward could directly be related to their pituitary's ability to produce endorphins. During World War II, 20% of the people who survived the horrors of concentration camps remained composed despite the constant physical, mental and spiritual deprivation. Hope, faith, and belief in a way of escape were the common denominators found among those who survived with a healthy state of mind. The other survivors, comprising 80%, still suffer today with health problems. "In returning and rest shall you be saved, in quietness and confidence shall be your strength." Isaiah 30:15.

Corrie ten Boom writes of her personal experience with recovering victims of concentration camps and the physical consequences of not forgiving. "I knew forgiving not only as a commandment of God, but as a daily experience. Since the end of the war I had had a home in Holland for victims of Nazi brutality. Those who were able to forgive their former enemies were able also to return to the outside world and rebuild their lives, no matter what the physical scars. Those who nursed their bitterness remained invalids. It was as simple and horrible as that."

MAINTAINING GOOD HEALTH

In 1975 I was hurt in an automobile accident. It resulted in my head being thrown through the driver's side window with my face being badly ripped by the broken glass. I was conscious, without pain, and calmly aware of my circumstances. An emergency medical technician was driving by and stopped to bandage me and summon an ambulance. My injuries involved my neck, face and teeth, all of which I could not see. The accident occurred at 3:00 P.M. and the plastic surgeon operated at 9:30 P.M. For those six and one half hours I waited, without pain, to have my neck and face stitched with 120 stitches. Four teeth were broken and had to wait three months to be repaired because of the neck injury. At the time I was thankful and amazed that I did not need any pain medication except for the Novocain administered during the stitching process. The glass-inflicted cuts were jagged and irregular, so the doctor had to cut skin and enlarge the wounded area in order to close the wound properly. One scar goes from one ear, under my chin, and to the other ear. At the time of my car accident I did not have any knowledge of endorphins and their effects, but I did trust in Divine Power. Now I realize my endorphin production must have been working overtime, just as God intended it to work.

Even though some of David Livingston's deductions were untested in light of the current information on endorphins, his account in 1850 of his encounter with a lion exemplifies the body's ability to automatically compensate for extreme stress and pain. "I heard a shout. Starting and looking half-around, I saw the lion just in the act of springing upon me. I was upon a little height; he caught my shoulder as he sprang, and we both came to the ground below together. Growling horribly close to my ear, he shook me as a terrier does a rat. The shock produced a stupor similar to that which seems to be felt by a mouse after the first shake of the cat. It caused a sort of dreaminess in which there was no sense of pain nor feeling of terror, though quite conscious of all that was happening. It was like what patients partially under the influence of chloroform describe, who see all the operation, but feel not the knife. This similar condition was not the result of any mental process. The shake annihilated fear, and allowed no sense of horror in looking around at the beast. This peculiar state is probably produced in all animals killed by the carnivore; and if so, is a merciful provision by our benevolent Creator for lessening the pain of death."

The implications of these scientific and personal observations are enormous for each person whether sick or well, nursing or ailing. How we think and treat one another has a tremendous effect on our peace of mind and on the serenity of others. How can we affect our endorphin levels? Negative thoughts and fears are known to depress endorphin levels, while thoughts of hope, assurance and redemption enable people to cope with painful situations. Irregularity in eating and sleeping have a negative effect on endorphin levels. An overworked stomach from too much food eaten too often draws on the brain's nerves and energy. Alcohol, tobacco and coffee sap brain power. Opiate centers crowd out endorphins by hooking up to the receptors reserved especially for endorphins. On the positive side is the fact that a diet high in carbohydrates will produce high levels of endorphins. This means fruits, nuts, seeds, grains, and vegetables.

Temperance in all things, deep breathing, correct habits of eating and drinking, all go to nourish the brain. Physical exercise and useful labor relieve a wearied mind. Sunshine and cool air uplift those who are fatigued by too much brain work. Listening to harmonious and melodious music and sweet and simple singing will elevate and ennoble the thoughts. The eight laws of health are potent antidotes to relieveng pain.

It is important to remember that pain, in reasonable levels, is an essential body protector. Our pain receptors remind us to pull our hands away from fire. One of the tragedies of leprosy is the effect the disease has on nerve endings. A leper looses pain sensations and consequently injures himself without realizing it. Successful leper programs recognize this phenomenon and make protective compensations.

Pain indicates a problem, but drugs mask pain symptoms. There are alternative natural remedies for pain. Cold compresses on sprains, and sutures during the first twenty-four hours after an accident or operation, are alternatives to pain medication. Hot and cold fomentations are effective for relieving pain by increasing circulation. Charcoal poultices reduce pain. Charcoal tablets, purchased in pharmacy or health food stores, can be crushed in a glass bowl to make a powder, or activated charcoal powder may be purchased. Add a small amount of water to make a paste and spread it on a gauze or cotton sheeting. Place the poultice on the painful area and cover with a piece of plastic bag to induce warmth and protect clothes and linens from charcoal stains. I have used charcoal poultices successfully with tooth pain, earaches, and gout, as well as upset stomachs.

A hot foot bath is a remedy for headache pain. Soak your feet in hot water for twenty minutes, replenishing the water to keep it hot. Ice or a cold cloth to the forehead and the hot foot bath work together to draw away congestion from the head. Several natural remedy books by Drs. Agatha and Calvin Thrash are listed in the bibliography and have proven to be indispensable to me in helping myself and my family with itches, cuts, aches and pains.

Many Bible verses encourage me to maintain an attitude of calmness and joy despite the otherwise stressful circumstances that might surround me. "Rejoice in the Lord" Philippians 4:4. Rejoice evermore. In everything give thanks" I Thessalonians 5:16,18. "Fear not little flock" Luke 12:32. "Count it all joy" James 1:2. Let not your heart be troubled" John 14:1. "All things work together for good" Romans 8:28. Remembering Bible verses, singing hymns, and trusting in Divine Power have brought serenity to many undernourished war prisoners shut away from sunshine and fresh air and deprived of proper rest, exercise, shelter and clothing. Even though they could not choose to experience the other seven laws of health, their faith in Divine Power gave them strength to endure. Think of peace of mind as a gift waiting to be unwrapped. You have to unwrap the package in order to enjoy the gift. The repercussions have immediate as well as eternal implications.

References:
1. "Brain Drugs Kill Pain," *Science Digest*, July 1983, pp. 141 - 142.
2. Cousins, Norman, *An Anatomy of an Illness*, Norton, NY, 1979.
3. Davis, Joel, *Endorphins*, The Dial Press, Garden City, NY, 1984.
4. Facklam, Margery and Howard, *The Brain*, Harcourt Brace, NY, 1982, pp. 55-61.
5. Janov, Arthur, *Prisoners of Pain: Unlocking the Power of the Mind to End Suffering*, Anchor Press, Garden City, NY, 1980.
6. Johnson, Timothy, *Harvard Medical School of Health Letter Book*, p. 102.
7. Lucinda, Frank, "A New Attack on Alcoholism," *New York Times Magazine*, October 20,1985, pp. 45 - 50.
8. Restak, Richard, MD, *The Brain,* Bantam, NY, 1984, pp. 158 - 170.
9. Ten Boom, Corrie, "I'm Still Learning to Forgive," *Guidepost's Treasury of Hope.*
10. White, Ellen G., *Education*, Pacific Press, Mt. View, CA, 1903, p. 197.
11. Id., *Testimonies to the Church*, Vol. 1, Pacific Press, Mt. View, CA, 1948, pp. 577,618.
12. Id., *Testimonies to the Church*, Vol. 2, Ibid., p. 531.
13. Id., *Testimonies to the Church*, Vol. 3, Ibid., pp. 152,157.
14. Id., *Testimonies to the Church*, Vol. 4, Ibid., pp. 31,515.
15. Id., *Testimonies to the Church*, Vol. 7 Ibid., pp. 256 - 257.

Researching
Your Allergy

Personal Inventory

As a result of the problems of eczema, nasal congestion and poor digestion, I have spent a lifetime in search of physical, mental and spiritual well-being. My eczema problem was eventually traced to wrong choices on my part. Peanut butter, lettuce, dates, and tomatoes as well as soil, grapevines, mold, and commercial cleaning combinations triggered the itch and scaling on my right hand. The nasal congestion was grain and dairy related and seasonally influenced. Add to this slow digestion and sensitivity to gas producing foods and you have a challenging case study. Learning to make thoughtful choices has been essential in my retaining good health.

My problems are not life-threatening, just life-annoying. Using elimination, rotation, and trial and error testing of food and nonfood substances, I have become more aware of my body's ability to deal positively or negatively with what I eat, touch or breathe. After forty-eight years of environmental annoyances, I can make a list of offenders, tack it up, and be reminded to avoid these things.

Clearness of mind and wellness of body are my health goals. The more I am in tune with my body's messages, the better I feel. I cannot afford an allergist, so I read, ask questions, listen, and experiment, and I have been finding answers. I choose not to use drugs because I believe that, in a life-annoying problem, drugs only mask the symptoms. With allergies it is important to keep the annoyances or pain out front. Awareness of the problem is the first step toward clarification.

In my search for health I found four sources to be especially helpful. I recommend them as priority reading. First, the Bible gives me faith that "I am fearfully and wonderfully made" (Psalms 139:14). God designed our bodies to fight disease. As we follow wholistic life-style principles set forth in the Bible,we can believe in the body's self-healing ability. Second, the writings of Ellen G. White, *Ministry of Healing* and *Counsels on Diet and Foods*,give a model to aim for in diet, healing, education, recreation, and Christ-centered menaality. Thirdly, clinical ecologist Dr. Theron Randolph has written a practical guide for people with allergies. In *An Alternative Approach to Allergies*, Doctor Randolph presents simple yet explicit directions in self-diagnosis and healing. Fourth, *The Healing Heart,* by Norman Cousins, gives scientific confirmation to the Biblical assurance that the human healing system is designed to be its own physician. Add to this quality nutrition and a positive attitude and it adds up to preventive medicine. Faith in the body's healing mechanism works closely with discernment and choice. Being informed, the second step towards comprehension, has given me greater control over my own health.

Allergists base much of their diagnosis on a patient's case history. Allergies are like fingerprints; there are no two alike. I wrote my own case history, and you can too. This was an opportunity to detach myself objectively from my problems as I viewed the total picture. I also experienced a positive relief and acceptance of my allergies through the process of expressing myself on paper. A case history consists of three basic forms: autobiography, a dietary history, and a life-style timeline. First I wrote an autobiography with the following headings: prenatal, birth, childhood, adolescence, young adult, middle age, and senior years. Under each heading I included information on eating, sleeping, exercise, recreation, study and spiritual habits, as well as illnesses, allergies, acute health problems, and causes of death in blood relatives. See charts in this section.

Second, I kept a dietary diary for a seven-day cycle, recording foods eaten and the times at which I ate them. Third, I wrote a detailed life-style timeline for a seven-day cycle, charting my rising and sleeping times, eating, study and recreation times. I took these three forms, autobiography, dietary diary, and life-style timeline, and studied them for patterns, repetitions and irregularities. This helped me to pinpoint problem areas. Dr. Randolph and Ellen G. White's books were helpful in giving me a model to aim for. Claiming God's promises gives me power to apply these practical principles and procedures to my own situation.

As I share my experience, you will see more clearly the place of these diagnostic techniques. In January 1981, the eczema on my right hand became a medical problem, as the open sores, caused by my scratching the irresistible itch, had begun to smell. I am a Seventh Day Adventist Christian, and my church has acute care centers worldwide, as well as small health-care institutes dedicated to using natural remedies for healing. I contacted my friends at Living Springs, a health-care facility in Putnam Valley, New York, and described my symptoms. It was explained that the smell was an indication of infection. The remedy recommended was to soak my hand in a charcoal bath four times a day for twenty minutes each time. I dissolved two tablespoons of crushed charcoal in a pan of hot water and as I slipped my hand into the pan I could feel the healing process at work. After two baths the odor was gone and my hand was on its way to healing, thanks to charcoal's amazing adsorptive qualities and infection-fighting ability.

The eczema was only a symptom, like the stuffy nose or itching skin. I wanted to find the cause. So I wrote my personal case history. As I studied my autobiography I saw a definite allergic tendency throughout my life. At birth I was sustained by soy milk formulas because of allergies towards cow's milk, which still exist. Childhood earaches, tonsillectomy, and at twelve a trip to an allergist, pinpointing sensitivity to wool and dust, illuminated the trend of my body's inability to deal with different substances. During young adulthood I supported several over-the-counter antihistamines in order to find relief from nasal congestion. At twenty-seven I acted upon a suggestion to drop dairy products, and was breathing freely -without drugs - within two weeks. I also went on a two-meals-a-day plan, with five hours between and no snacking, and found my digestive problems relieved. After a few spoons of ice cream, with a headache and stuffy nose following, I was convinced that the taste was not worth the pain. As with alcohol, tobacco and caffeine, I realized the negative effects were not worth the initial experience.

At thirty I became a vegetarian, abstaining from all animal products, except honey on an occasional basis. I became committed to the Eight Laws of Health, as written in Ellen G. White's *Ministry of Healing*. Each day I found time for quality nutrition, exercise, water, sunshine, temperance, fresh air, and trust in the Lord, and my itching and sneezing abated.

Two years later the nasal congestion manifested itself, and my five year old son was plagued with earaches. The search for food allergies began again. After a two week elimination diet of eating only two or three different foods at each meal, we began to experiment. First we eliminated wheat and found relief within a few weeks. We each had been eating four to six slices of homemade whole-wheat bread a day. The next winter he had no earaches and my nasal congestion was gone.

With no bread, pasta and crackers, alternatives had to be found. There are a variety of grains such as millet, buckwheat, rice, oats, barley, rye, and corn. In my ignorance I emphasized oats, rice, and corn for their taste and workability. So, when in January of 1981 the eczema on my hand became infected, I had to continue the search. It was at this point that I read Doctor Randolph's book and realized the mistake I had made in eating the same foods all the time, thinking it was safe for me to do so. From my dietary history I could see a strong emphasis on the same grains, fruits and vegetables, though I never ate beans because of their gaseous qualities. It made even more sense as a christian to take advantage of the wide variety of foods that God has created.

After a three-month elimination diet, I began to introduce possible offending foods gradually and my hand and nose became the testing ground. When I ate oat, rye, barley, rice or corn I sneezed and sneezed within two hours. Peanut butter, dates, tomatoes, blueberries, and lettuce made my hand itch with red hives. I also experimented with vitamin supplements, but because of my wheat and rice allergy I couldn't find any that I could tolerate. I was at the point of dreading mealtime for fear of reactions that might follow.

A rotation diet, as described in Doctor Randolph's book, brought stability out of confusion. On a rotation diet I have a specific weekly food menu. Every day is preplanned. I rotate my menu on a four-day cycle, not eating the same foods within these four days. The meals in general are simple, using only one or two combinations. It is a challenge and a blessing to be a cook-chemist, experimenting for myself, my three children and husband. Organization and preplanning are keys to success. I apply the same principles to the family members without allergies as a preventive measure. For example, we will have brown rice, black beans, tacos, popcorn, and broccoli for a main meal. Simplicity at each meal and variety over the week is an important principle. I rotate the type of spreads I use, such as almond butter, homemade sugarless jams, and tahini, on millet crackers or buckwheat waffles. Breakfast cereal is topped with a different milk made from sunflower seeds, almonds, soy, or cashews, and sweetened with banana, carob or apples. By trial and error experimentation I have found that I can tolerate split peas and lentils in the morning, so I now can glean their valuable nutrition. Gluten grains are a fixed allergy for me, they always offend. My immune system seems to be rebuilding resistance because I can eat rice, millet, buckwheat and quinoa more often than on a four day rotation and I'm not limited to only eating them in the morning as I once was. Dates, tomatoes, blueberries, and lettuce no longer cause hives or itching. I still only occassionally eat peanut butter as I break out on my face when I use it too often. I have, however, found a wide variety of fruits, vegetables, seeds, and nuts that satisfy my hunger and appeal to my tastes.

Having a goal, faith, knowledge, and thoughtful choices have been essentials in overcoming my allergy problems. Applying these four principles has been crucial and challenging. I can honestly say that I am thankful for my allergies because I have reaped a healthful diet, clearness of mind, and an opportunity to share my experience in hopes that it can be of service to others.

Most allergy cookbooks that I have read use rice and oats as a replacement for gluten grains. Refined sugars, fats, and processed foods are also commonly used in allergy recipes. To survive, I have developed child-tested recipes and used them successfully while teaching natural food cooking classes, and at family and church functions, and even as successful entries in cooking contests. All recipes are wheat-free, egg-free, dairy-free, and sugar-free.

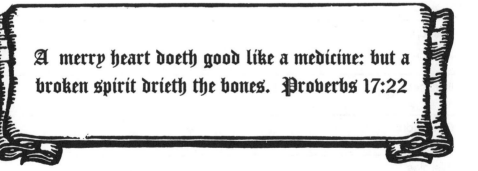

A merry heart doeth good like a medicine: but a broken spirit drieth the bones. Proverbs 17:22

Case History—Autobiography: Report anything that has had a physical, emotional or mental effect on you. List any foods, beverages, chemicals, places, or activities you believe to be significant. Note any health problems.

Experiences Habits	Prenatal	Birth	Infancy	Childhood
Eating				
Drinking				
Sleeping				
Exercise				
Recreation				
Smoking				
Study Habits				
Spiritual Habits				
Illnesses				
Operations				
Allergies				
Annoyances				
Alcohol or Drug use				

Case History—Autobiography: Report anything that has had a physical, emotional or mental effect on you. List any foods, beverages, chemicals, places, or activities you believe to be significant. Note any health problems.

Experiences:

Habits	Adolescence	Young Adult	Middle Age	Senior Citizen
Eating				
Drinking				
Sleeping				
Exercise				
Recreation				
Smoking				
Study Habits				
Spiritual Habits				
Illnesses				
Operations				
Allergies				
Annoyances				
Alcohol or Drug use				

Case History—Ancestral History

	Mother	Father	Sister	Brother
General Health Analysis Excellent- Fair- Sickly-				
Acute Health Problems				
Annoyances: itches, rashes, headaches, congestion, fatigue				
Allergies: sinus, hay fever, asthma, eczema, air pollution, cleaning products, yeast infections				
Causes of Death: Natural, heart attack, accidental, cancer				
Smoking Habits: Never- Started what age? Stopped what age? Still smoking				
Alcohol Consumption: Special Occasions-moderate, daily, habitual, excessive?				

Case History – Ancestral History

	Paternal Grandmother	Paternal Grandfather	Maternal Grandmother	Maternal Grandfather

General Health Analysis
 	
Excellent-
  Fair-
    Sickly-				

Acute
  Health
    Problems				

Annoyances: itches, rashes, headaches, congestion, fatigue				
Allergies: sinus, hay fever, asthma, eczema, air pollution, cleaning products, yeast infections				
Causes of Death: Natural, heart attack, accidental, cancer				
Smoking Habits: Never- Started what age? Stopped what age? Still smoking				
Alcohol Consumption: Special Occasions- moderate, daily, habitual, excessive?				

Case History—Time Line: Work, study, recreation, spiritual time, rising and bed time, and liquid intake (amount and time).

	Sunday	Monday	Tuesday	Wednesday	Thursday	Friday	Sabbath
6:00 a.m.							
7:00 a.m.							
9:00 a.m.							
10:00 a.m.							
11:00 a.m.							
12:00 noon							
1:00 p.m.							
2:00 p.m.							
3:00 p.m.							
4:00 p.m.							
5:00 p.m.							
6:00 p.m.							
7:00 p.m.							
8:00 p.m.							
9:00 p.m.							
10:00 p.m.							
11:00 p.m.							
12:00 a.m.							

Case History—Food Diary: Note food, amount and time eaten.

		Breakfast	Lunch	Supper
S U N D A Y	Main Dish: Second Dish: Raw: Bread: Spread:			
M O N D A Y	Main Dish: Second Dish: Raw: Bread: Spread:			
T U E S D A Y	Main Dish: Second Dish: Raw: Bread: Spread:			
W E D	Main Dish: Second Dish: Raw: Bread: Spread:			
T H U R S	Main Dish: Second Dish: Raw: Bread: Spread:			
F R I D A Y	Main Dish: Second Dish: Raw: Bread: Spread:			
S A B B A T H	Main Dish: Second Dish: Raw: Bread: Spread:			

Rotation Diet and Meal Planner

Learning to live with your allergies is a challenge and can be a blessing. Though you may have "fixed" allergies to some foods, and you will have to eliminate them from your diet permanently, there will be other foods you can reintroduce on a rotating basis. A four-day rotation is minimal, and some may find seven or fourteen-day rotations to be more effective.

Once you have determined the foods to which you have sensitivities, the next step is to avoid these foods for five days, several weeks, or up to three months to give your body a chance to clear itself from any annoying symptoms. When the symptoms disappear you can begin to reintroduce the foods and observe your reactions. Your reactions will determine if these foods can be used on a rotation diet.

Rotation or rotary diets are suggested by doctors for those who cannot afford testing or don't want to subject themselves to skin-testing needles. Many doctors believe that 80% of allergy symptoms could be reduced by rotating foods, according to *The Allergy Self-Help Book* by Shawn Faelton. One of the reasons adverse symptoms occur is due to the gradual buildup of antibodies that cause the reactions. According to *The Allergy Self-Help Book*, rotating foods will allow your antibody levels to subside.

When setting up a rotation diet, one needs to take into account likes and dislikes as well as offending foods. Make a list of all the foods which you can eat without adverse reaction and enjoy them. It was once thought that you needed to rotate your foods within food families. For instance, if you discover an allergy to soybeans, then it would be recommended to eat only legumes once every four days. Usually this is unnecessary, according to recent research reprinted in Rodale Press's *Allergy Relief Newsletter* of February 1988. Here it states that only the offending foods need to be strictly eliminated or rotated.

Learning about food families is a challenge, due to some commonly misunderstood relationships. For instance, peanuts are not nuts but part of the legume family. White potato is a nightshade, along with peppers, eggplant and tomatoes; however, it is not related to the sweet potato at all. Cucumbers are part of the squash family, as are melons. Botanists classify all seed-bearing plants as fruits, while agriculturists consider fruits as ever-bearing trees or berries grown in an orchard, and vegetables as mostly annuals grown in the garden. The source of your information will influence how you classify foods. People who have nightshade intolerance usually are allergic to all nightshades; however, this is not a hard and fast rule with other food families, except with the crustacea family (shrimp, crab, and lobster). Each of us are individuals, and food families may or may not be an issue in our allergy picture.

Seasonal considerations can also be important. During ragweed season many find that melons give them a negative reaction, whereas during other seasons melons can be eaten without any problems. If you have an increased level of mucous during the change of seasons, you might try eliminating wheat or oats, which tend to be mucous-forming. Eliminating or rotating mucous-forming grains during a cold may also be helpful. A firm principle for rotating diets is adding variety to your food choices. Variety over the weekly menu and simplicity within each meal will help you to avoid developing future allergies. Choose three or four foods in as natural a state as possible and fill up on these at mealtime. Avoid complex mixtures at each meal. Make up for variety in foods with variety in texture. Use corn in soy-corn cakes, popcorn and corn on the cob at the same meal. Use millet as your bread, with millet sticks, millet in your dessert, and in place of rice for your grain dish. Fresh apples, APPLESAUCE, APPLE FLAT CAKE, and BAKED OATMEAL make for simple and interesting breakfast.

Another important tool is to keep an account in a journal of the foods you eat and your reactions. In time you will be able to set up a schedule with which you will be comfortable. The goal is to become familiar with your body's reactions to foods and environmental influences. As you listen to your body's messages you will become better acquainted with your allergy picture. These messages will help in your recovery. Chart out a menu schedule to help you be consistent with your rotation diet, and post it in a convenient spot as a reminder. Make several copies of the blank sample menu plan following this article and experiment with food combinations to find the best plan for you. Some will have to be more rigid while others will be able to be more flexible.

In reviewing the rotation diet, first eliminate offending foods and when symptoms disappear reintroduce the problem food, rotating that food over at least a four-day period. Keep your menu simple for each meal and varied over the week. Inform yourself about food families to see if you have multiple allergies within a family. Keep a food diary and note physical and emotional reactions to the foods you eat. Make a menu plan focusing on your individual needs.

References:
1."Allergy Update: Don't Put Too Much Stock In Food Families, " *Rodale's Allergy Relief*, February 1988, Vol. 3, No. 2, p. 7.
2.Crook, William, *Tracking Down Hidden Food Allergy*, Professional Books, P.O. Box 3494, Jackson, TN, 38301.
3.Faelton, Shawn, *The Allergy Self-help Book*, Rodale Press, Emmaus, PA, 1983.
4.Mandel, Marshall, MD, *Five Day Allergy Relief System*, Alan Mandell Center for Bio-Ecologic Diseases, Norwalk, CT.
5.Randolph, Theron, *An Alternative Approach to Allergies.*
6.Thrash, Agatha, MD, and Calvin, MD, *Food Allergies Made Simple,* Family Health Publications 13062 Musgrove Hwy. Sunfield,Mi. 48890

Learn for yourself what you should eat, what kinds of foods best nourishes the body and then follow the dictates of reason and conscience."
Ellen G. White, Healthful Living, p. 76.

Weekly Meal Planner: Breakfast, Lunch, or Dinner

	Sunday	Monday	Tuesday	Wednesday	Thursday	Friday	Sabbath
Main Dish							
Second Dish							
Raw Dish							
Whole Grain Bread							
Gravy, Spread, or Nuts							

Sample Weekly Menu

		Breakfast	Lunch	Supper
S **U** **N** **D** **A** **Y**	Main Dish: Second Dish: Raw: Bread: Spread:			
M **O** **N** **D** **A** **Y**	Main Dish: Second Dish: Raw: Bread: Spread:			
T **U** **E** **S** **D** **A** **Y**	Main Dish: Second Dish: Raw: Bread: Spread:			
W **E** **D**	Main Dish: Second Dish: Raw: Bread: Spread:			
T **H** **U** **R** **S**	Main Dish: Second Dish: Raw: Bread: Spread:			
F **R** **I** **D** **A** **Y**	Main Dish: Second Dish: Raw: Bread: Spread:			
S **A** **B** **B** **A** **T** **H**	Main Dish: Second Dish: Raw: Bread: Spread:			

Yeast and Allergies

Candida albicans belongs to the yeast family of simple cell fungi. Fungi, which are part of the plant kingdom, live everywhere - in the air, in the soil, and in our bodies. The most familiar fungi are mushrooms, baker's yeast, brewers yeast, torula (food) yeast, penicillin, mold and mildew. Thousands are present in a handful of soil. Rust and smut fungi infect trees, plants and grain crops. Ringworm of the scalp and athletes foot are caused by fungi. Glycerin, vitamins, citric acid, vinegar, and alcohol are all by-products of yeast fungi. People eat fungi in the form of roquefort and camembert molds on cheese. Enzymes of fungi are used in food processing. We are surrounded by fungus. Presently there are more than 100,000 different types, but every year new species are classified.

Yeasts are parasites that get their nourishment from living on or in plants and animals and they thrive in warm, damp environments. One of the problems with Candida yeast allergies involves the unique conditions under which yeast organisms reproduce. This persistent yeast lives in the mucous membranes of the human body, especially in the digestive tract, intestines, and vaginal area. Candida yeast is greedy and will eat any substance containing starches or sugars. This yeast multiplies as its food source is increased. This increase comes from our eating refined carbohydrates whose sugar content is rapidly digested and overloads the blood witP the Pugar the yeast craves. Such things as sugar and honey sweetened treats, white rice and white bread and pastries have this effect. Diet plays a crucial role in controlling Candida yeast infections.

A diet of unrefined carbohydrates, such as whole grains, beans, vegetables and fruits, are usually tolerated by the yeast-sensitive person because these foods digest gradually and the blood stream is not overwhelmed with sugars. The presence of fiber in whole foods helps to regulate the breakdown of nutrients at a pace which the body chemistry understands.

A healthy immune system and the presence of beneficial bacteria also help to keep yeast in check. Bacteria are as numerous in the air, soil, water, and human body as fungi. There are harmless, beneficial and also harmful bacteria. You are no doubt familiar with pneumonia, TB and tetanus as harmful bacteria, but without beneficial bacteria in the human digestive tract food residues would not be broken down to harmless waste products. Compost piles depend on beneficial bacteria to convert kitchen wastes, grass and leaves to soil. Beneficial bacteria are normal residents of our body habitat, and one of their jobs is to keep yeast organisms under control. Antibiotics destroy friendly as well as harmful bacteria indiscriminately and yet do not bother the yeast at all. With the bacteria killed off by the antibiotic, the Candida yeast organisms are left free to multiply. Since antibiotics have come into such widespread use in the past 10 years, Candida infections have proportionately increased.

The immune system is weakened also by a diet high in refined carbohydrates. White blood cells, the soldiers of the immune system, are overwhelmed by the same overabundance of sugars that the Candida feeds on. It appears that toxins are released from the yeasts as they multiply and these toxins circulate throughout the body, impairing the immune system. Yeast allergies result from a vicious cycle of dietary abuse of sugar and refined foods and the overuse of antibiotics, hormones or cortisone-type drugs, yeast overgrowth, a weak immune system, and sensitivity to the ever-present fungi family.

It has been difficult to test for Candida overgrowth because the organisms are normally present in everyone. Scientists are researching in this field to find a specific diagnostic measure to pinpoint Candida infection. Although a very good blood test is now available for chronic yeast infection, it is quite expensive and requires a physician to draw blood and send it to an appropriate laboratory. Until better diagnostic tests are found, analyzing your case history to connect life-style choices with symptoms, applying appropriate treatment, and positive responses to these treatments, are ways to identify a yeast allergy. Symptoms of fatigue, depression, skin problems, stomach irritations, vaginitis, hyperactivity, headaches, and stuffy nose conditions have all been connected with the overproduction of Candida. These symptoms and combinations of symptoms are symptomatic of other medical problems as well. As any illness usually has a variety of interrelated causes, it takes patience and thoughtful trial and error efforts to pinpoint Candida's cause and effect patterns.

In his book, *The Yeast Connection,* Doctor William Crook recommends that if you suspect yeast allergies, first go on an elimination diet that is yeast-free, sugar-free, fruit-free, refined grain-free, nut-free, and milk-free. When your symptoms improve or go away, which is usually in 5 to 10 days, you can slowly begin to reintroduce different foods and watch for symptoms. Doctor Crook suggests that you use eggs, fish, meat, and vegetables with the exception of potato and sweet-potato when going on his initial elimination diet. For the vegetarian and those concerned with the disease found in animals, meat is an objectionable source of nutrition. The main dishes section of this cookbook offers a variety of protein recipes using a combination of tofu, beans, whole grains, and vegetables as alternatives to flesh foods.

If you prove to be sensitive to yeast, a maintenance diet should eliminate all dairy products, yeast-raised breads, Brewers yeast, alcoholic beverages, malt products, foods containing vinegar, processed and smoked meats, fruit juices, coffee, tea, melons, mushrooms, refined sugars, peanuts, packaged and processed foods, hormones, antibiotics, and corticisteroids.

There are foods which inhibit Candida growth. Be sure to include at least one serving of the following each day: broccoli, onions, turnip, kale and cabbage. Garlic, on a daily basis, can be an alternative to Nyastatin, a drug often used to control Candida. Doctor Agatha Thrash, in her book *Food Allergies Made Simple*, suggests using dehydrated garlic tablets. Arizona National Products is a source of high quality garlic tablets; Garlicia, by Nature's Way, claims to have all the antibiotics and antifungal effects of fresh garlic.

Each person is a unique individual, so trial and error procedures must be patiently tested in order to develop a customized diet and life-style program. Positive results can take anywhere from several weeks, months, or in a rare few, even years of treatment. The principles of the eight laws of health are compatible and basic to any health program. A person with known or suspected yeast allergies will benefit from patient, careful attention to self-control in diet, exercise and deep breathing in the fresh air and sunshine, drinking proper amounts of water, proper rest, and especially in taking time to be in tune with their spiritual needs. The eight laws of health are enablers which strengthen the body systems to fight infections and disease.

References:
1. Crook, Dr. William, *The Yeast Connection*, Professional Books, P.O. Box 3494, Jackson, TN 301, 1983.
2. Kavaler, Lucy, *The Wonders of Fungi*, John Day Company, NY, 1964.
3. Kime, Zane R., MD, *Sunlight Can Save Your Life*, World Health Publications, Penryn, CA, pp 60-61.
4. Madlener, Judith Cooper, *The Sea Vegetable Book,* Clarkson N. Potter, NY, 1977.
5. Marx, Wesley, "Seaweed, The Ocean's Unsung Gift," *Reader's Digest,* June 1984, pp. 3948.

6.Thrash, Agatha, MD, *Food Allergies Made Simple*, Family Health Publications Sunfield, Mi. 36875.

7. Wollner, David, "Shoppers Guide to Natural Foods," *East West Journal,* Sept. 1981, pp. 38-42.

Arthritis-Nightshade Allergy

There are various alternatives for people who avoid peppers, eggplant and tomatoes because of arthritis -

• You can use JACK CHEESE with grated carrot instead of pimento   cheese.

• You can substitute zucchini for eggplant in recipes.

• You can make PESTO pasta. Put PESTO, (the recipe is found in Preserving Naturally), over spaghetti or layer with crumbled tofu and lasagna noodles for pesto lasagna.

Food Additives and Allergies

Food processing, longer shelf life, flavorings, appearance, consumer demand for convenience foods all have brought food adulteration to a point of concern for many who are sensitive to chemicals or yearn for pure and healthful foods. Natural, of course, is not a guarantee of safety. There are numerous poisonous plants that are natural but deadly.

Many food additives are listed on the GRAS list, Generally Recognized As Safe, by the FDA, the Food and Drug Administration, the governmental watchdog agency. A substance is considered unsafe if it has been shown to induce cancer in animals or humans according to the 1958 Delancy Clause of the Food, Drug and Cosmetic Act. Some of the safe additives have restrictions as they cause allergic reactions or cause problems if they exceed certain levels. For instance, sulfites are disastrous to those with asthma, causing hives, nausea, diarrhea, shortness of breath, and fatal shock. Although banned from use on raw fruits and vegetables in salad bars and grocery produce counters, sulfites are still sprayed on fresh grapes by the growers to lengthen shipping life. Growers are required to label at least 40% of individual branches of treated grapes. Sulfites are used in many packaged foods such as dried apricots, seafood, beer and wine.

Monosodium glutamate (MSG), according to FDA reports, is on the GRAS list because it "poses no health hazard to adults at percent levels of use." MSG is made from corn or wheat and may cause chest discomfort, headaches and tingling of fingers and toes to hypersensitive persons. FDA officials believe that only a minority have allergic reactions and that adequate labeling alerts the sensitive individuals. The FDA receives 12,000 to 15,000 consumer complaints concerning allergic reactions per year. Seventy percent of these are food related. One must be prepared to be a label reader as well as being willing to write to manufactures and question what their products are made of and inquire as to percentages of ingredients.

Some chemicals are used in the processing of food but are not listed on ingredients lists. For instance, methylene chloride is used in the decaffeinating process of coffee but has been banned from use in aerosol hair sprays as it has caused tumors in laboratory animals. Methylene chloride is allowed to be used in the decaffeinating process as long as levels do not exceed ten parts per million.

Some chemicals are by-products of the cooking process. There is as much benzopyrene, a carcinogen related to stomach cancer and leukemia, in a 2.2 pound charcoal-broiled steak as the smoke from 600 cigarettes. The fat from the steak drips on the charcoal, forming the toxic chemical.

Salt and sugars are by far the additives used the most in processed foods. Again, the minority suffer outwardly the ill effects of excess. The healthy consumer, however, profits from awareness of the amounts and uses of salt and sugars in processed foods. Aspartame, commonly known as Nutrasweet, continues to be a controversial additive, as does the irradiation process for preserving foods. Other concerns are with coal tars and artificial colorings used in ice cream, candy, Jell-o, nuts and hot dogs. Nitrates, BHA, BHT and saccharin are other additives that are controversial. Your evaluation as to the harm or merits of food chemicals depends on the sources you read.

The issue of chemicals in foods is broad, controversial and changing. The consumer is faced with taking personal responsibility for finding out about the uses and effects of chemicals to be able to make intelligent decisions when purchasing foods. The FDA justifies its policies as the best for the majority and attempts to protect the minority rights with careful labeling legislation and ongoing testing. Consumer advocates, such as Ralph Nader, Micheal Jacobsen, Beatrice Trum Hunter and Jacqueline Veret, believe the federal agencies could do more to inform and protect the public. That there is a battle going on over chemicals in food preservation and production is not in question. The problem is who you believe.

By growing your own foods, eating foods as grown and cooking from scratch, you can avoid the additive issue. However, if you choose to buy processed foods, eat in restaurants, or your children eat at school cafeterias, you might want to read labels, research and ask questions. Be informed and keep up to date as to the changes in the food processing business.

References:
1. Brody, Jane, "Food Additives, Do They Hurt?", *New York Times,* section c1, pages 8,10, July 12, 1978.
2. "Chemical Cuisine" poster available from the Center for Science in the Public Interest, 1755 S Street NW, Washington, DC 20009
3. Hunter, Beatrice Trum, *Consumer Beware,* Simon and Schuster, NY, 1971.
4. Hunter, B. T., "Food for Thought: Aspartame," *Consumers Research,* January 1986, pp. 22-25.

5.Hunter, B. T., "Food for Thought: All Natural; " *Consumers Research*, April 1987, pp. 8-9.

6.Jacobson, Micheal, *Eaters Digest: The Consumer's Factbook of Food Additives*, Doubleday: Anchor, NY, 1972.

7.Lecos, Chris, "Sweetness Minus Calories = Controversy," *FDA Consumer*, February 1985.

8.Lecos, Chris, "Cancer, The Law and Methylene Chloride," *FDA Consumer*, March 1986.

9."News Digest: Sour News; New Evidence Sours Nutrasweet, *"Vegetarian Times*, November 1987, pp. 8-9.

10.Scharffenberg, John, MD, *Problems With Meat,* Woodbridge Press Publishing Company, Santa Barbara, CA, pp 32-33.

11.Schmid, Judith, "The Additives Debate," *Vogue,* October 1987, pp. 405:486-487.

12.Segal, Marion, "A Potpourri of Consumer's Questions About Food," *FDA Consumer,* November 1987, pp. 30-32.

13.Thrash, Agatha, MD, and Calvin, MD, *Nutrition For Vegetarians*, Lifestyle Books, Seale, AL, pp.83-85.

14.Turner, James, *The Chemical Feast.* Ralph Nader's Study Group Report on the Food and Drug Administration, Grossman, NY, 1970.

15.United Press International, "Too Much Nutrasweet: Factor in Behavior, Birth Problems," *Keene Sentinel,* April 29. 1987, p. 12.

16.Verett, Jacqueline and Carper, Jean, *Eating May Be Hazardous to Your Health*, Anchor Books, Garden City, NY, 1975.

17.Winter, Ruth, *A Consumer's Guide to Food Additives*, Crown Publishing, NY, 1974.

Learning to Live
with
Your Allergy

Modifying Recipes

One of the best tools for the person with food allergies or sensitivities is to learn how to modify existing recipes. A minority of my recipes are original. The majority are modifications of existing recipes. Even the originals were inspired from foods I wanted to eat but could not.

Over the years I have accumulated files of newspaper and magazine clippings and xerox copies of recipes. To the best of my knowledge I have contacted all those whose recipes I have used verbatim, or modified, and want to extend my appreciation to each of the authors of the cookbooks listed below for their allowing me to use their recipes. My intent has been to provide those suffering from food allergies with a starting point, and as each reads they will in turn be inspired to experiment. Please feel free to write and let me know about your successes.

My Cookbook Library:

1. Allen, Earl and Dotty, *Newstart Homestyle*, Box 486, Weimar, CA 95736.
2. Bauer, Cathy,*The Tofu Cookbook,* Rodale Press.3. Beltz, Muriel, *Cooking With Natural Foods*, Black Hills Health & Education Centre, Box 1, Hermosa, SD 57744.
4. Calkins, Fern, *It's Your World Vegetarian Cookbook,* Review & Herald Publishing Association, Washington, DC, 1981.
5. Cottrell, Edyth, *Oats, Peas, Beans & Barley,* Woodbridge Press, PO Box 6189, Santa Barbara, CA 93111.
6. Country Life Nutrition Seminar, Newton, NJ.
7. Dameron, Peggy, *The Joy of Cooking Naturally*, Box 3368, Bauman, CA 95604.
8. Earl, Evelyn, *Something Better Cookbook*, Amazing Facts, Frederick, MD 21701.
9. Hagler, Louise, *Tofu Cookery*, Book Publishing Co., Summer Town, TN.
10. Hurd, Rosalie, *TenTalents,* Book 86A, Route 1, Chisholm, MN 55719.
11. Peters, MD, Warren, *Hartland Heartsavers,* Box 1, Rapidan, VA 27733.

12. Rachor, JoAnn, *Of These Ye May Freely Eat*, Family Health Publ., 8777 E. Musgrove Hwy., Sunfield, MI 48890.
13. Robertson, Laurel, *Laurel's Kitchen*, Ten Speed Press, Berkeley, CA.
14. Shurtleff, William, *The Tofu Book,* Ballantine Books, NY, 1981.
15. Thomas, Anna, *Vegetarian Epicure*, Vintage Books, NY, 1972.
16. Tadej, Lorine, *Strict Vegetarian,* MMI Books, Harrisville, NH 03450.
17. Thrash, MD, Agatha, *Eat For Strength,* Uchee Pines Inst., Seale, AL 36875.

Substitution Chart

SUBSTITUTE	INSTEAD OF	TO USE AS
Agar Agar	Jell-o	thickener
Almonds	dairy	milk
Apples	pectin	thickener
Apple juice	sugar	sweetener for jams
Arrowroot	flour or cornstarch	thickener
Bananas (frozen)	dairy	ice cream
Bananas	eggs	binder
Barley Malt	sugar	sweetener
Bragg's Liquid Aminos	soysauce	seasoning
Buckwheat Noodles	wheat	spaghetti
Carbonated Mineral Water	soda	fizz
Carob	chocolate	sweetener
Cashews	dairy	milk, cheese
Chicken Style Seasoning Homestyle	packaged seasonings	seasoning
Corriander	cinnamon	seasoning
Corn flakes	breadcrumbs	binder
Cumin	chili	seasoning
Dates	sugar	sweetener
Emes Kosher Gelatin	Jell-o	thickener
Fruit, fresh and dried	sugar	sweetener
Grain Beverage Caffix,Pero,etc.	coffee	beverage
Honey	sugar	sweetener
Fruit Juice Concentrate	sugar	sweetener
Lemon Juice	vinegar	salad dressings, pickling
Millet	butter or margarine	base
Mung Bean Thread	wheat	spaghetti (cellophane noodles)
Pineapple juice	sugar	syrup for canning
Potato starch	flour	thickener
Soybeans, soaked	baking powder	leavening
Sunflower seeds	dairy	milk, salad dressing
Tahini	oil	salad dressing
	eggs	binder
Tapioca cornstarch,	flour	thickener
Textured Tofu Protein	TVP	non-meat extender
Tofu	cheese	cottage cheese
	dairy	ice cream
	eggs	scrambled
	eggs	tapioca pudding
	mayonnaise	salad dressing
	meat	protein

Environment and Allergy Response

Traveling has given me a perspective on my allergies and confirmed the cumulative and saturation aspects of allergic reactions. A weak immune system can tolerate just so much. In reviewing the cause of an allergic reaction you might pinpoint a certain food you are sensitive to; but also consider air pollution, lack of sufficient sunshine, contact with harsh household chemicals, or stress. Your body's defense system can become overwhelmed.

I lived in northern California between September and April, 1973-74, when I gave up dairy products. After two weeks of avoiding dairy products I didn't have any nasal drip or sneezing or headaches. This lasted for the nine months that I spent there. We should not minimize the effect of sunshine, fresh air and exercise as healing agents.

I spent the spring and summer of 1974 on the mid-west coast of Michigan and continued to enjoy good health. I attribute this to my vegetarian diet, daily outdoor walking and gardening exercise, and abundance of local produce and fruit. The end of May we enjoyed local asparagus; in June, strawberries and cherries; July, fresh garden vegetables; August, apricots, peaches, plums and blueberries; and September, apples and pears. I can close my eyes and envision the many peaceful hours spent in garden, orchard and field picking God's gifts. What a balm to a diseased body and mind to climb trees, hoe weeds, search out the hidden blueberry, transplant strawberry runners, or harvest and shell fresh garden peas.

While living in the northwest corner of New York's Catskill Mountains between 1980 and 1985, my nasal cavities were challenged to filter out smoke from the two wood stoves which had to burn for 9 months out of the year, and mildew and mold from a damp mud-floored basement. In 1985, I lived in a damp basement in western Connecticut and had a different internal body response after learning the importance of keeping the drip trays and filters of air conditioners, humidifiers, or dehumidifiers clean. if these filters are dirty they will introduce mold spores into the circulated air and cause havoc in sensitive nasal cavities. When living in the Catskill Mountains, March and August marked the hay fever season. In September of 1985, the hurricane Gloria triggered my worst attack of hay fever while living in the southwest corner of Connecticut.

LEARNING TO LIVE WITH YOUR ALLERGY

Spending September through November of 1984 in dry, sunny Southern California, I didn't suffer nasal problems except when I spent too much time inside a centrally air-conditioned home. An abundance of sunshine, minimum of smog, and plenty of outdoor time gave my whole system relief. The desert's lack of greenery is not as pleasing to the eye as the green hills of the Catskills, but to my nasal cavities the dry desert sun brought relief. Added to this was a reasonable and abundant supply of fresh fruits, vegetables and nuts. This is my personal experience, but some generalizations may be gleaned. Allergies have an cumulative effect and the weak immune system reaches a saturation point. The key is to create for yourself an environment attuned to your strengths and weaknesses. Country living should be a top priority. Daily outdoor exercise is a must. Careful attention to what you eat, touch and breathe can mean the difference between allergic reactions and contentment. Approach a problem with a willing and teachable spirit. Often it is impossible to move from a troublesome environment, as each person s situation is unique; but you should do the best you can with what you have. Inquire, explore, experiment, think and reason for yourself. Blessings will come from your efforts.

Stand ye in the ways and see, and ask for the old paths, where is the good way, and walk therein and ye shall find rest for your souls. Jeremiah 6:16

Growing Your Own Herbs

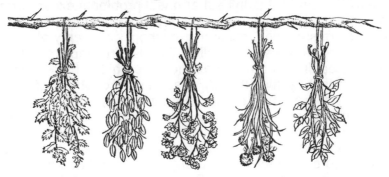

Natural foods have delicate flavors. Some people have described the flavors of whole grains and beans as earthy and bland. You can liven up the taste of your whole-food recipes with herbs grown in your own outdoor, indoor or porch garden.

Certain herbs are easier to grow than others; many perennial herbs grow like weeds. You will never regret setting off a special spot in your flower garden for perennial herbs or filling in spots in your vegetable garden with annual herbs. My teenage son and I rehabilitated a section of pasture turned forest, and the rich loam was perfect for growing herbs. If you live in the city or have limited space, herbs do well in pots, bushel baskets, wooden fruit boxes, or even an old pail with holes drilled in the bottom. I have even used a discarded wooden animal trough.

My first herb experience was with basil and dill. Basil is an annual, so you can sow the seeds directly in the garden in the spring of each year. Italian basil, sweet basil and purple basil all grow well in most soil conditions, but will be fuller and bushy in rich humus fertilized soil. During the summer, snip basil leaves for fresh tomato sauce or pesto. Throughout the summer snip off and discard the flowering center to encourage further bushy growth. In the early fall cut the stem close to the ground and hang the plant upside down to dry in a dry, dark or filtered light area.

Dill is a prolific herb as well. In spite of below zero winters in the Catskills of New York, volunteer dill popped up in the spring from stray seeds of the former season's plants. Add dill seeds and fresh chopped onions to Sumerian barley flat bread for a pleasing taste treat. Dill's tall growth may give it a back row place in the garden, but it will give your potato salad or your pickled cucumbers a first place vote from your family.

Be patient with parsley. These tiny seeds can take up to two weeks to germinate in the soil. Once parsley takes hold it is hardy and, because it is a biannual, you can enjoy parsley in early spring if you are careful not to plow your summer plants under. As a good source of iron, parsley and pineapple juice blended in your blender make a nutritious and refreshing drink.

Sage and catnip grow easily from seed sown directly in the garden. Use starter plants or garden cuttings of thyme, chives and marjoram to fill out your perennial garden. Space your plants well, as these herbs will expand. Chives grow so well that you will enjoy sharing clumps each spring with your friends. One of the pleasures of gardening is the blessing of watching perennial plants multiply, digging them up, dividing, and sharing or replanting the harvest. Garlic chives or Egyptian onion chives offer a stronger taste than chives. Any of these three are delicious when added to scrambled tofu, providing just the flavor to add zing to an otherwise neutral tofu taste. An extra added bonus is to pick the pink chive flowers and dry them for a winter bouquet. Dill heads, thyme and marjoram flowers, and sage leaves are all usable for dried flowers. Sage and thyme give beans a hearty flavor.

The self-propagation powers of herbs, such as sage, is a wonder to me. You can plant 2 or 3 small plants of each herb and the next year your garden will be full and in need of dividing and replanting.

Various members of the mint family, such as catnip, lemon balm, pineapple mint, apple mint, spearmint, and peppermint, are all easy to grow and provide for sturdy plant structure. My children love to pick the lemon balm leaves and then chew them for a quick mouth refresher. Iced mint teas can be summertime coolers. Grow a good amount of catnip, wait until it flowers, then pick the plants and dry them and you will have a natural, simple remedy on hand when you need a relaxant, throat soother, or sleep inducer.

To dry your herbs, cut the stems close to the ground after flowering has taken place and tie them in bunches with wire wrap or rubber bands. Hang them in a dry place. My nasal cavities do not appreciate herbs or flowers drying inside our house. I used the attic and the back wall of our garage as drying areas. If you can tolerate the odors, pollen and spores, the kitchen can be a wonderful place to dry herbs.

When the herbs are dry, use a large brown paper bag as a collector. You can cut the bag and spread it on the floor or use it intact. I gently push my fingers down each stem to force the leaves and flowers to fall on or into the bag. Then I gather up the herbs and store them in glass jars or plastic bags.

Rosemary and bay are attractive and useful house plants. Check with a local nature center or herb society for sales. The best sources for herbs usually are fellow gardeners. My knowledge of herbs expanded by my encounter with Jan Green, a professional flower designer, who grew her herbs in the Catskill Mountains and sold her wreaths and baskets of dried flowers and herbs in New York City. Jan started me out with my first herb garden in the spring of 1981 as she divided overgrown plants, and, as we traded her herbs for my whole grain baked goods, we became good friends.

Gardening is a wonderful way to relax and ease negative stress. The therapy found in digging in the soil is beneficial to both mind and body. If you are allergic to soil molds, use cotton gloves to protect your hands. I have a stash of white cotton gloves from my mother's senior citizen friends who have cleaned out their glove drawers. If you are looking for a fulfilling gardening experience, try experimenting with herbs!

Camping With Whole Foods

How to achieve the simplicity necessary for a camping menu, yet have a variety of wholesome food is easier than you may think. Camping food doesn't only have to rely on canned goods. Good entrees can be split pea soup or lentil soup. At home, grind up some lentils or split peas in a dry blender and pack in plastic ziploc bags. Cooking time is thus shortened to one-half to three-quarters of an hour instead of 1 1/2 to 2 hours. Bring along dried onion, garlic, rosemary powder, and salt for seasonings.

Other good entrees can be created by using Textured Tofu Protein (TTP). Freeze a pound of drained tofu in a plastic bag.

Defrost and drain in a colander. To speed up the process, you can run hot water over the frozen tofu or put in microwave for 3 minutes at medium. Squeeze out all of the water and then crumble the tofu on a cookie sheet. Dry at 200°- 250° until tofu becomes crunchy. You can store it in a plastic bag. One pound of tofu will yield one cup of TTP. To re-hydrate, add 1 cup of water to 1 cup of TTP. Use it to make anything for which you would use hamburger or TVP. Substitute it for meat in Sloppy Joe's. Saute an onion in a frying pan and add TTP and tomato sauce and serve hot over buns or zwieback.

Vegetable combinations are good as camping main courses. Boil potatoes and onions until tender; then drain and add a can of green beans and season with salt. You can even sprout alfalfa seeds in a plastic bag with holes in the bottom when you go camping. Don't forget to rinse and drain each day.

Desserts can be carob peanut butter balls or puffed cereal

candies. Add 1/4 cup honey, 1/4 cup carob, 1/2 cup peanut butter, 1/4 cup coconut, and 1/4 cup sunflower seed meal or dry milk powder. Mix all the ingredients well and then form into small balls with your hands. To make puffed cereal candies, mix 1/4 cup of honey, 1/4 cup of peanut butter or tahini, and 2 tablespoons of carob powder until the mixture is creamy; then add enough puffed millet or rice cereal and coconut to prevent stickiness. Also, refer to the Preserving Naturally section for making your own fruit leathers.

Breakfast is easy with ready-made granola or puffed whole grain cereals topped with dates, raisins, or nuts and moistened with unsweetened canned fruit. Popcorn is a good evening meal. Zwieback (twice baked bread) and whole grain crackers can be made ahead of time, and will not mold as bread will. To make zwieback, slice your bread, lay the slices on a cookie sheet, and dry in your oven at 250° with the oven door ajar to let moisture escape. The process generally takes about two hours.

Camping can be a wonderfully whole experience. Camping in the open air affords us the opportunity to take advantage of all the 8 laws of health.

Holiday Menu

Tofu Rice Loaf	Cashew Gravy
Cranberry-Pineapple Sauce	
Sweet Potatoes	Peas and Onions
Popcorn	Pineapple Butterfly
Date Nut Bread	Apple-Date Pie

Thanksgiving is traditionally a time of celebration for the fruitful harvest. Today it has become a holiday of over-abundance. Science has found that excess intake of food or drink on a regular basis is correlated with disease. Excess of calories leads to obesity. Excess of fat leads to atherosclerosis. Excess of sugar leads to diabetes or hypoglycemia.

Excess of refined products leads to constipation and diverticulitis. Excess of alcohol leads to cirrhosis of the liver. Reasoning from cause to effect, we can see abstinence from harmful food and drink and moderate but sufficient intake of good foods equals health.

The food we prepare and eat at Thanksgiving time can mirror the sentiments of the celebration. Gratitude for the blessings of the year, and a spirit of sharing the excess that we have, rather than consuming it ourselves, can give us a true spirit of thankfulness. The Bible suggests that when we have a feast we are to go out to the highways and byways and bring in those in need.

The Pilgrims celebrated the first Thanksgiving in 1620 in thankfulness for a bountiful harvest, after spending a previous winter near to starvation. This was not really the first Thanksgiving. The Bible explains that the Israelites celebrated an annual Feast of the Tabernacles to thank God for their bountiful harvest and the future harvest of God's people through the Messiah.

Thanksgiving traditionally pivots around the turkey, stuffing, gravy and pumpkin pie, because these were the foods available to the Pilgrims. Today a wide variety of foods are available. Unlike the Pilgrims, we are able to make choices dependent on quality rather than availability.

Above is a low fat, low sugar, no cholesterol holiday menu suggested from recipes in Taste and See.

The No Itch, No Sneeze Birthday Party

Allergies are like fingerprints, there are no two alike. My teenage son, Joshua, has struggled with dairy- and wheat-related allergies his whole life. The struggle is with the reactions to eating the offending foods and with the deprivation of the traditional foods such as bread, pasta, and sweets made with dairy and/or wheat products. Sneezing and stomach cramps are overt symptoms when he indulges in the forbidden foods. The problem is life-annoying, not life-threatening, but the fact remains that it is a difficult choice to turn down a piece of birthday cake or an ice cream cone.

Finding delicious and healthful alternatives has been a challenge and a blessing. It has meant starting new traditions which have been spilled over to relatives and friends. Birthdays at our house are special occasions because the birthday person chooses the menu for the day. Usually breakfast is banana splits with a choice of toppings. The main ingredient for the banana split is cooked whole grain cereal. Oatmeal or millet are good choices because they stick together and can be molded with an ice cream scoop. The children enjoy creating their own inventions with homemade carob topping, strawberries, blueberries, crushed pineapple, chopped nuts, coconut, granola, and almond cream to top it off. What fun to compare each original plateful.

The principle behind replacement is **Something Better.** By offering tasty alternatives cake and ice cream can be satisfactorily replaced. Frozen carob-covered banana Popsicles take the place of ice cream. Strawberry ice, peach-cashew ice cream, or pineapple sherbet are other nondairy options. Nut cups, dried fruit balls or carob peanut butter balls are candy's proxy. Table decorations are edible butterflies or candles fashioned from pineapple rings and other dried and fresh fruits. The pineapple ring cut in half and decorated with raisins becomes the wings. The abdomen is a date and the antennae are sliced apricot strips. The candle is made with a pineapple ring as the base and a quarter of a banana stuck into the center as the candle. The flame placed on top of the banana can be either a strawberry or cherry. The cake is replaced with an apple flat cake made with oats and fresh grated apples and raisins. Joshua can also choose from sun bars or sesame squares as sweet grainless treats.

Birthdays are a time for thankfulness at our house. The children become givers as well as receivers. Any kind of disability can draw undue attention to self, so we attempt to draw our children's attention towards service for others. We encourage the children to give of themselves on their special day. We plan to give a helping hand to an elderly neighbor or make special birthday treats and share them with friends.

Balloons and games are appropriate, but the theme is cooperation rather than competition. A pre-lunch peanut hunt is always a success. Pin the cabbage in the patch, or the carrots in a row, or the beans on a pole, rather than sticking the abused donkey with pins. A fun take-home project for the guests would be a sprouting kit. Joshua assembles the kits out of wide mouth quart canning jars and adds a piece of nylon screening five inches by five inches and samples of alfalfa and mung bean seed with a set of instructions.

Getting the children involved is a successful approach to acceptance of iew and different foods. Joshua has been making granola and bread since he was three. When his sister, Amber, was six, and his brother, Noah, four, they took over these jobs, and Joshua graduated to desserts and entrees. CAROB PEANUT BUTTER, FROZEN BANANA POPSICLES, and SESAME FINGERS are two of his specialties. He successfully entered the Oneonta, New York, Daily Star Bake Off and won tenth place in 1983 and fourth place in 1984. He was competing against 400 entries and fourteen finalists. This positive reinforcement has been an encouragement that being different can also bring rewards.

Education is another key to acceptance of new foods. As the children learn about their bodies' nutritional needs, and their positive and negative reactions to certain foods, they begin to understand the reason behind healthful choices. Eating choices can be controlled by the mind rather than the sometimes fickle senses. It is difficult at best for adults to practice self-control in the hundreds of sugar-laden and fat-soaked delicacies. Learning temperate habits while young lays the foundation for thoughtful choices throughout life and gives better odds to living a longer and more abundant life. Our allergy experiences have been a blessing because in our search for alternatives we have found the treasures of better health, both of body and mind.

The Eight Laws Of Health - Child Style

Let us pretend we are going on a train ride through the countryside. We will ride on a special train called the Healthland Flyer. The different places that you will visit will remind you of ways to help your body and mind to be healthy and happy.

Before the journey starts, the engineer needs help to inspect the brakes and the throttle. The engineer has to go over his Control Check Chart before the train goes on a journey. When the brakes go on, say "Psst." When the throttle goes on, pull your hand back. Check the brakes, "Psst." Did you make the brake noise? Check the throttle. Did you pull your arm back? Boys and girls need to know when to put their brakes on too. There is a time to play, a time to work, and a time to rest each day. There are times to say "No, thank you," when offered food, drink or anything that might hurt us. Do you check your Control Check Chart each day?

Now that the train checks out, it is time to start. The conductor calls "All aboard! First stop, GOOD FOOD TOWN."

Climb the steps into the passenger car and find a seat. The conductor needs help pulling the whistle cord. The whistle blows when the train leaves a station and when the train is coming into a station.

Toot! Toot! Pull the imaginary chord for the train will soon be taking off!

Pull the throttle! Use your hands to make quiet wheel motions. Off we chug!

The conductor is coming around to collect the tickets. The ticket you need to ride on the Healthland Flyer is a willing heart and mind to think and to do.

As your quiet wheels chug down the track, you can see apple orchards on each side of the tracks. See the grape vineyards and vegetable gardens. There is an almond orchard too!

Toot! Toot! The train whistle is signaling that the train is coming into GOOD FOOD TOWN. The wheels slow down.

Push the throttle.

"Psst" go the brakes.

Let us get off the train and enjoy a walk through the orchards. Do you have a favorite fruit or vegetable? Tell me what it is! Have you ever grown your own garden or gone to an orchard or berry patch to pick fruit?

I hear the conductor calling "All aboard!" Let's head back to the train.

Toot! Toot! The train is ready to start. Next stop is FRESH AIR HOLLOW. We will go through SUNSHINE VALLEY. We can sit in this open car and enjoy the warm and healing rays of the sunshine.

Pull the throttle!

Keep the quiet wheels turning!

Even on cloudy days we can share sunshine by sharing smiles with everyone we meet. A smile is like a ray of sunshine. A smile can turn a grumpy heart into a happy heart!

Toot! Toot! We are coming to FRESH AIR HOLLOW.

Push the throttle forward to stop the train.

"Psst" go the brakes.

After we get out we can practice deep breathing exercises. Remember, breathing from your abdomen is best. Put your left hand on your side just above your waist. Feel for your last rib bone. Place your right hand on your stomach. In between is your diaphragm. This is where your breathing action should be. Take a deep breath, pushing out your stomach area. If your shoulders move, you need to practice abdominal breathing.

"All aboard," the conductor calls.

Let us get back to the train!

Pull the whistle cord. Toot! Toot!Pull the throttle and off we go, heading for CLEAR WATER FALLS. You can see the clear sparkling river flow along and hear its sweet babbling song.

Toot! Toot! The train whistle blows!

We will stop ahead to take a water break.

"Psst" go the brakes!

Careful as you jump off the train!

The water cascades down the rocks to form a quiet pool for us to drink from. We can drink this water right from the stream. So refreshing! Just what I needed to quench my thirst!

"All Aboard!"

Time to get back on the train.

Toot! Toot!

Pull the throttle!

Turn the quiet wheels and we are chugging off up LONG REST MOUNTAIN.

There is a tunnel ahead. The tunnel goes right through LONG REST MOUNTAIN. We can close our eyes and rest for awhile as we travel through the tunnel. It is dark in the tunnel, but I see a ray of light ahead. Not far past the end of the tunnel is our next stop!

The conductor calls, "Next stop, CLIMB A HILL JUNCTION!" I am looking forward to exercising. My legs get stiff if I sit too long. Look! We are passing over RUN AND JUMP HIGHWAY. See the people briskly walking. Their cheeks are rosy and they are smiling. Wave back to the friendly walkers!

Toot! Toot! We are coming into the station!

"Psst" go the brakes!

Push the throttle to stop the engine!

Let's get out and take a walk up the hill. Walk in place as you pretend to climb. We'd better head back down the hill as it is getting close to train time. I hear the whistle -Toot! Toot! "All aboard!"

Pull the throttle and here we go!

Start your quiet wheels moving again. Last stop will be THANKFULNESS SQUARE.

This is my favorite stop. This little town helps me to remember to count my blessings. Do you have something you are especially thankful for today? I am thankful that God made so many wonderful helpers to keep me healthy. I am thankful for good food, sunshine, fresh air, clean water, time to rest, time to work, and reminders to say "No, thank you" so I can stand up sor what is right. Why do we need to take care of our bodies anyway? Why is it so important to visit these special health spots each day? We want to be healthy and happy so we have more energy to help others. Helping and happiness go together.

Toot! Toot! The whistle tells us it is time to head back!

"All aboard for the express train back to your homes," calls the conductor.

To get the train moving pull the throttle!

Chug! Chug! The quiet wheels are turning!

Wave goodbye to THANKFULNESS SQUARE and we are

heading towards CLIMB A HILL JUNCTION. Wave to those smiling folks walking on RUN AND JUMP HIGHWAY. Exercise really makes their faces glow! I see LONG REST MOUNTAIN ahead. That means we will be going through the tunnel. Here it comes! This will give us another chance to take a rest. Out into the sunshine and I see a rainbow over CLEAR WATER FALLS. I am thankful I learned deep breathing exercises at FRESH AIR HOLLOW. SUNSHINE VALLEY is such a bright and cheerful place to travel through. Here come the gardens of GOOD FOOD TOWN. When I get home, I think I will start my own garden. I can stay healthy by getting exercise digging in the soil and enjoying the fresh air and sunshine at the same time. I know I will be thankful for all the good food that will grow from the seeds I plant. I will be better able to say "No" to junk food if I can go pick my own treats from the garden.

The station is ahead.

"Psst" go the brakes.

Push the throttle!

The wheels stop.

I am sorry to end this journey!

You can ride on the Healthland Flyer anytime. Every day visit all the special places and you will be healthy and happy and willing to share your happiness.

The Lego® Toy Immune Army-Child Style

To make the work of the white blood cells more concrete in a child's mind, you can stage a simulated battle using Lego toy men to impersonate the body's true soldiers. The phagocyte unit of granulocytes and macrophages can be represented by Lego Castle soldiers with red armor and black and grey helmets, shields and weapons.

The T cell division of helper T cells, killer T cells, suppressor T cells, and memory cells can be depicted by Lego white, red, yellow and black space astronauts. The concept of the B cell, which turns into different cells in the war process, can be better understood by using a plain Lego knight as the B cell. Add a helmet to represent the B cell turned into a plasma cell. Add a feather to the helmet to represent the plasma cell produced antibody. As an antibody the knight with helmet and feather is ready to start the complement connection. The Lego space laser gun placed on the knight's hand represents the connection point for the complements. Nine green and red Lego extension pieces are then added to the gun to represent the complements 1 through 9. This complement gun provides the antibody with the power to detonate and blow the enemy all apart.

As you set up the battle, display a group of enemy cells represented by extra Lego workmen. Give names to the enemies, such as germs and poisonous chemicals. Designate a spot for the lymph nodes, thymus and spleen where the killer T cells, suppressor T cells, memory and B cells can wait for the helper T cells to report to them as to the battle plans. The granulocytes, macrophages and helper T cells will be at the battle site ready to attack and report back for reinforcements.

Use your imagination and this opportunity to familiarize your children and yourself with the intricate plan behind the immune system's strategies.

Hints For Better Digestion

Some allergies result from improper digestion. Chunks of undigested food may be considered an antigen (an unknown enemy) by the body's immune mechanisms. The body will go into motion to get rid of the antigen and will either over-react or under-react, causing an allergenic response.

• Chew your food well. Remember, digestion begins in the mouth as your saliva mixes with your food. Gas is often caused by unmasticated food.

• Regularity in eating gives your stomach the necessary time schedule for work and rest. Eating two or at most three meals a day, 5 to 6 hours apart, allows the digestive organs to digest one meal completely, and then rest before it starts on another meal. Foods you get a reaction from may be better digested in the morning at your first meal of the day. High protein foods, such as beans and nuts, are better digested at the morning meal.

• Simplicity at each meal is important in aiding digestion. Two to four combinations of food is enough at one meal. Generally it is best not to eat fruits and vegetables at the same meal. Experiment on yourself because each person is unique as to their digestive capabilities. I am able to digest beans and fruits at breakfast. I can also mix bananas, dates or pineapple with certain vegetables at my second meal. Remember that to one person wheat may be a wholesome food and to another wheat may be a troublemaker.

• Rotation of troublesome foods on a four-day basis may allow you to tolerate foods you otherwise would avoid. Some foods are fixed allergies. No matter when you eat them your body reacts negatively. For myself, dairy foods, wheat, rye and barley are consistent in their negative affect. I can rotate peanut butter, dates and tomatoes and get along fine. Occasionally I can eat rice and oats without too adverse a reaction. By experimentation I have found that I cannot tolerate any grain at my second meal or I will wake in the night with nasal congestion. Again, each person is an individual and can experiment and uncover the best individualized diet for themselves.

• Moderation is a principle of digestion. Overeating taxes the digestive organs. Your organs will react to food overload in the short range by gas or indigestion, and in the long range by obesity and eventual shutdown of the pancreas, gall bladder, liver and intestines.

• Drink only water between meals and avoid drinking any liquids with your meal. Liquids dilute the stomach digestive juices resulting in longer digestive times and incomplete digestion.

• Moderate exercise in the fresh air and sunshine aids digestion.

Reminders and Review

1. Start your day with a substantial **BREAKFAST.**

2. Eat a wide **VARIETY** of foods throughout the week.

3. Practice **SIMPLICITY** at each meal, using no more than four different types of food.

4. **ROTATE** your food choices. Allergies often originate from foods eaten too often.

5. Eat **WHOLE FOODS.**

6. Eat at **REGULAR** hours with no in-between-meal snacks.

7. Eat with **GRATEFULNESS.**

8. Drink 6-8 glasses of **WATER** per day.

9. **EXERCISE** in the fresh air and sunshine each day.

10. Foster a sense of **HUMOR.**

11. **HELP** at least one person each day.

12. Treat yourself to a regular daily **QUIET TIME -** study, pray, meditate, and recharge your physical, mental and spiritual capabilities.

Recipes

Breakfast Foods

BREAKFAST FOODS

Better Breakfasts

"Fill-up." When one starts on a car trip, one of the first things to do is to fill up the gas tank. Each morning we begin a journey, an adventure of experiences and encounters. Begin each day with an adequate breakfast. Fill up for optimum performance.

"Eat like a king at breakfast, a prince at lunch, and a pauper at supper" is a wise saying. Ask yourself these questions: Does your body need the most calories at the beginning or end of the day? When are you most active? The majority of Americans eat their biggest meal in the evening even though their activity level lessens to a slower pace. It makes more sense to eat a good-sized breakfast to give your body the needed fuel and building blocks for a full day's activity.

Studies show that children perform better in school after a good breakfast, and lower grades correlate with poor breakfast eaters. There are more accidents with factory workers who eat an insufficient breakfast.

What is a good breakfast? Fill up with a balance of carbohydrates, proteins, vitamins, and minerals, but keep fat and sugar levels low! - a main dish of whole grains such as cornmeal, millet or rye cereal, a fresh fruit or two, whole wheat bread or crackers, and a cooked fruit. A meal of granola with milk or fruit sauce topping, two slices of whole grain bread and a fruit or nut spread, a banana and an apple, is a quick but nourishing breakfast. The majority of time spent will be in chewing.

Use a crockpot to cook your cereals on low, overnight. Make waffles ahead of time, freeze them, and warm them up when needed. Navy beans over toast or a bowl of split pea soup make for a fulfilling winter breakfast.

Children will be more willing to eat a bowl of hot cereal if you dress it up with a fruit face of raisin eyes, a banana mouth, and coconut hair. Try an oatmeal banana split. Use the cereal in place of ice cream and have a variety of toppings for the children to choose from. Coconut, nuts, pineapple, fruit sauces, and granola are possible toppings. Substituting cooked cereal for dry boxed cereal will be a bargain as well. Breakfast can be the best meal of the day as well as the most nourishing.

CROCKPOT CEREAL
Yield: Serves 4-6

What You Need

1 cup barley, pearl or whole
7 cups water
1 t salt
3/4 cup slivered or chopped
  almonds (optional)

1/2 t ground coriander, optional
1 1/2 cups chopped dried mixed
  fruit (apples, pears, raisins,
  dates)

What You Do

1. Toast almonds in oven at 250° about 15 minutes.
2. Place barley and water in crockpot set at low and cook all night.
3. Add remaining ingredients, except almonds, about 30 minutes before serving in the morning.
4. Just before serving, sprinkle with toasted almonds.
*Variation: Use whole oat groats or rye berries.

BAKED OATMEAL
Yield: serves 4

What You Need

4 cups dry oatmeal
3/4 cup raisins
1/2 t salt

6-8 cups water (less for quick
  more for thick rolled oats)
1/2 cup coconut

What You Do

1. Sprinkle raisins evenly on the bottom of an 8 x 12 baking dish.
2. Sprinkle oatmeal evenly on top of the raisins.
3. Sprinkle coconut evenly on top of the oatmeal.
4. Sprinkle salt evenly over ingredients.
5. Add water and cover. Bake in oven for 1 hour at 350°.

SIMPLE GRANOLA
Yield:10 cups

What You Need

7 cups rolled oats
1 t salt
1 cup DATE OR RAISIN
   BUTTER

1 cup dried, unsweetened
   coconut
1/2 cup sunflower seed meal
1 cup water or pineapple
   juice

What You Do

1. Blend sunflower seeds in a dry blender to make meal.
2. Mix oats, coconut, sunflower seed meal, and salt.
3. Add date butter and water to dry ingredients.
4. Mix well.
5. For crunchy granola use more liquid. For flaky granola use less liquid.
6. Divide onto 2-4 cookie sheets.
7. Dry in oven at 200-250° for 1 1/2 hours. Stir every 15 minutes.
8. Consider the reliability of your oven temperature and be on the lookout for overbrowning. Scorched or burnt grains should not be eaten as they would be suspected of being carcinogenic.
9. The granola will be done when the majority of grains are golden brown. It will get crisper when it dries.
10. Remove from oven and let cool.
11. You can add raisins or nuts at this point.
12. Store in an air-tight container.
13. Use as a topping, cereal or base for granola crust. It is always good for camping breakfasts softened with fruit juice.

*Variation: Substitute rice flakes, barley flakes or rye flakes in place of the rolled oats.

AKORA GRANOLA
Yield: 3 cups

What You Need

4 cups akora (Akora is the leftover residue from the tofu production process. A source would be a tofu producer.)
1/2 t salt

1/4-1/2 cup sweetener (honey will make a lighter colored granola, molasses or barley malt will make darker granola)

What You Do

1. Mix ingredients well.
2. Spread out on oil-less cookie sheets.
3. Bake in oven at 250° for 2 hours.
4. Stir every 1/2 hour until dry and crispy.

SOY-OAT WAFFLE
Reprinted from the *Oats, Peas, Beans and Barley Cookbook*
Yield: 2 waffles

What You Need

2 1/4 cups water
1/2-1 cup soaked soybeans

1 1/2 cups rolled oats
1/4 t salt (optional)

What You Do

1. Soak soybeans overnight in sufficient water to cover.
2. Drain and discard water. (Soaked soybeans covered with water may be kept in your refrigerator for a week, or frozen.)
3. Combine all ingredients and blend until light and foamy.
4. Let stand while waffle iron is heating, batter will thicken.
5. Re-blend until creamy.
6. Oil waffle iron and follow directions for waffle iron. Takes about 10 minutes per waffle.
*Variation: Replace soaked soybeans with 1/2 lb. tofu.

APPLE PIE WAFFLE
Yield:2 waffles

What You Need

3/4 cup almonds
3/4 cup coconut
6 T potato starch
2 - 3 cups water
1 t coriander

1/4 t salt
1 t vanilla
1/2 cup grated apple
2 T tahini if not Silverstone
    or Teflon waffle iron

What You Do

1. Combine all ingredients except the grated apple and blend smooth adding water to make thick but pourable batter.
2. Fold in grated apple.
3. Preheat waffle iron and oil well. Cook 10-15 minutes.

BUCKWHEAT-SOY WAFFLES
Yield: 2 waffles

What You Need

1 cup soaked soybeans or soaked garbanzos or 1/2 lb. tofu
1 cup buckwheat groats   2 cups of water

What You Do

1. Soak 1/2 cup soybeans or garbanzos overnight in two cups of water and drain before using.
2. Blend all ingredients in blender until creamy.
3. Oil waffle iron. Preheat. Bake 10-15 minutes.
*Variation: Sprinkle sesame seeds on top of batter before you close waffle iron to cook.
*Suggestion: Leftover soaked soybeans can be refrigerated, covered with water, or drained and then frozen. Look for raw buckwheat that has not been roasted. The taste is milder. Usually available at health food stores.

BREAKFAST FOODS

BUCKWHEAT COCO-SUN WAFFLES
Yield: 2 waffles

What You Need

1 cup buckwheat groats   1/4 cup coconut
1/4 cup sunflower seeds   1/2 t salt (optional)
2-3 cups water

What You Do

1. Blend dry ingredients and 2 cups water in your blender.
2. Add additional water to make creamy, thickish but pourable batter.
3. Oil waffle iron and follow instructions for your waffle iron.
*Variation: For CAROB WAFFLE add 3 - 4 T carob powder and 1 ripe banana and increase water to make pourable batter.

GARBANZO COCO-SUN WAFFLES
Yield: 3-4 waffles

What You Need

1 cup soaked garbanzo   1/4 cup potato starch or
  or soybeans or 1/2 lb. tofu   arrowroot
3/4 cup sunflower seeds   1/2 t salt
3/4 cup dry coconut   2 T tahini (optional)
                                2-3 cups water

What You Do

1. Soak 1/2 cup garbanzos overnight in 1 1/2 cup water.
2. Drain, rinse, and drain again.
3. Blend all ingredients until smooth and creamy.
4. Add water to make thick but pourable batter.
5. Spray "Pam", or other non-stick cooking spray, on waffle iron.
6. Cook 10 minutes or until not sticking to iron.
*Variation: Replace garbanzos with quinoa or amaranth.

BREAKFAST FOODS

GRATED POTATO WAFFLE
Reprinted from the Amazing Facts *Something Better Cookbook*

While waffle iron is heating, grate 1 medium potato. Spray "Pam", or other non-stick cooking spray, on waffle iron. Spread grated potato evenly on waffle iron. Salt lightly. Cook 10-15 minutes. Makes a very crispy waffle.

RICE TOFU PANCAKES
Reprinted from *The Joy of Cooking Naturally Cookbook*
Yield: Pancakes for 2-3 hungry eaters

What You Need

1/4 cup sunflower seeds	1 1/2-2 cups of water
1 cup brown rice	1/2 t salt
1/2 lb. tofu	2 T sweetener (optional)

What You Do

1. Soak brown rice in 1 1/2 cups of water overnight.
2. Blend all ingredients in blender until creamy.
3. Add up to 1/2 cup of extra water to make proper consistency.
4. Oil griddle (If using Silverstone only oil once.)
5. Use 2 T each for half dollar sized pancakes or 1/3 cup for crepes.
6. Let bubble then flip and cook 2 minutes or until brown. Delicious with sugarless jam toppings or CAROB PEANUT BUTTER FROSTING or whipped tahini and banana slices.
* Suggestion:
a. If you forget to soak the rice you can put 1 cup of rice into 1 1/2 cups of water and microwave 5 minutes on high or put into a pot, cover and bring to a boil. Turn off heat and let set 5 minutes or substitute 1 cup of rice flour and eliminate step #1.
b. Substitute almonds or cashews for sunflower seeds.
c. Use batter to make waffles.

BUCKWHEAT TOFU PANCAKES OR CREPES
Yield: Pancakes for 2-3 hungry eaters

What You Need

1/2 lb. tofu
1 cup buckwheat groats

1 1/2 to 2 cups water

What You Do

1. Blend all the ingredients in a blender until creamy, add water if needed. The desired consistency is like pancake batter.
2. Bake on oiled pan by large spoonfuls for pancakes or by 1/3 cupfuls for crepe.

CREPE CAKE
Yield: serves 4-6

What You Need

10 RICE TOFU
  PANCAKES
12 dried apricots
10 nuts of your choice
1 cup ALMOND CREAM

1 1/2 cups APRICOT
  MARMALADE
1 20 oz. can unsweetened
  pineapple rings

What You Do

1. Place first crepe on a decorative plate.
2. Spread generously with apricot marmalade.
3. Continue to layer crepes and spread.
4. Decorate top layer with almond cream.
5. Grind or chop nuts and sprinkle on top.
6. Cut pineapple rings in half and decorate edge of cake with the 1/2 rings of pineapple and dried apricots.
7. Chill and serve.

BREAKFAST FOODS

EAST INDIAN DOSAS
Yield: serves 4

What You Need

1 1/3 cups cornmeal or
  buckwheat flour
2/3 cup rice, soy, or
  millet flour

1/2 t salt
2-3 cups of water

What You Do

1. Mix flours and salt.
2. Add water gradually to make pancake consistency batter.
3. Pour out on oiled griddle into silver dollar sized pancakes or crepe size (1/3 cup).

POTATO PANCAKE
Reprinted from *The Country Life Natural Foods Cookbook*

What You Do

1. Steam until tender 5 to 7 unpeeled potatoes. Leftovers may be used.
2. Peel and mash the potatoes then add remaining items:

1/2 cup soy milk
1 1 /2 t onion powder

1 t salt
3-4 T fresh parsley

3. Form into patties. Patties should be moist.
4. Place on well-oiled baking sheet.
5. Bake at 375° for 20-40 minutes, turning once.
6. The pancakes will form a brown crust.

EGGLESS FRENCH TOAST
Yield: enough for 6 slices

What You Need

2/3 cup water
1/2 cup tahini

1/4 t salt
2-3 pitted dates

What You Do

1. Blend smooth all ingredients.
2. Dip bread in mixture and bake on oiled cookie sheets at 350°
   for 15 minutes each side, or on oiled skillet.
3. Make thicker by adding more dates or tahini.
*Variation: For a bread substitute thaw frozen tofu, squeeze
excess water out of tofu, slice and dip in batter.

The Milk Myth

Do all children need cow's milk to grow strong bones and teeth? Is cow's milk good for everyone? Problems from milk drinking involve iron deficiency, anemia, allergies, early heart attacks, chronic cramps, and diarrhea. Over thirty million Americans are allergic to milk because of low levels of an enzyme called lactase in their intestines. The body will not digest lactose (milk sugar), unless sufficient amounts of lactase are present. At five years old the amount of lactase begins to lessen and by adulthood many loose the ability to produce lactase. Eighty percent of Japanese, Filipinos and Arabs have lactose intolerant reactions. Seventy to eighty percent of American blacks and Jewish adults cannot handle lactose digestion.

Cow's milk is nature's prescription for calves. Human breast milk is the ideal food for infants. Jane Brody, in her "Personal Health" column in the New York Times, proclaims the advantages of breast-fed babies. Cow's milk has four times more protein than human breast milk. This high protein, high fat content may be a step toward "over nutrition." As a rule, babies raised on cow's milk will weigh more than comparable age breast-fed babies. Breast-fed babies reach their optimum growth, but at a more desirable steady pace. Dr. William Stini, an anthropologist at the University of Arizona, explains "maximization of growth should not be confused with optimization."

Along with accelerated growth, cow's milk can cause digestive problems. Milk protein is 80% casein, which is harder for an infant to digest than the highly digestible whey protein which accounts for 70% of the protein in breast milk. Cow's milk protein is low in the amino acid cystine, which is essential to a newborn's diet, yet is high in the amino acid phenylalanine, which infants are unable to properly metabolize. Important antibodies are present in breast milk to protect the infants from infectious organisms. Doctors find that breast-fed babies have only a third as many serious illnesses as formula-fed babies during their first year of life. Breast milk is the perfect food for infants and is sufficient in essential nutrients until the time teeth begin to cut. Teeth cutting and saliva development indicate the presence of enzymes that enable the infant to digest starches. This age varies between 6 months and a year. Many allergies are the result of babies' immature digestive systems forced to improperly digest foods, which in turn causes flatulence, eczema, and other annoying symptoms.

The Committee on Nutrition of the American Academy of Pediatrics made the following statement: "It [cow's milk] is not an essential component of diet for everyone whose diet is otherwise adequate." If you don't get your calcium from cow's milk, what are the best sources? Calcium-rich plant foods include dark leafy greens, with 1 cup of collards higher in calcium than an equal amount of cow's milk. (Please refer to calcium chart.) Almonds, broccoli, tofu, sesame seeds, and garbanzos are all good sources of calcium.

How much calcium do we need? The Food and Agriculture Organization and the World Health Organization of the United Nations recommends 400 to 500 mg. of calcium per day for adults, while the United States daily recommendation is 800-1200 milligrams. Canada and England give 500 mg. as an adequate daily requirement. Malnutrition in the Third World countries are a result of insufficient calories rather than a specific vitamin or mineral deficiency. In a comparative study between the low calcium Bantu diet and the high calcium diet of Caucasians, Alexander Walker, head of the Human Biochemistry Research Unit of the South African Institute for Medical Research, found no evidence showing that calcium deficiency exists in humans. Even among populations that consume 400 to 500 mg. of calcium daily there are no major deficiencies.

Calcium malabsorption is more a problem in osteoporosis (bone loss) than of insufficient calcium. Doctor Morris Natelovitz, in his book *Stand Tall: The Informed Woman's Guide to Preventing Osteoporosis,* lists bone robbers and bone enhancers. Too much protein increases calcium excretion in the urine. Red meats especially promote excretion of calcium because of the acidic nature of the protein. The human body responds to acid overload by dissolving bone tissue as the body attempts to neutralize the acidic environment. The vegetarian's diet is low acid, while meat diets are high acid.

Salt is a bone robber; 200 milligrams of salt per day causes no change is calcium excreted, but use of 1 teaspoon (which is 2,000 milligrams of salt) shows increased calcium in the urine. Foods high in phosphorous - like soda pop, and processed foods that contain phosphorous additives, are bone robbers because, in order to absorb calcium properly, the body needs a 2 to 1 ratio of calcium to phosphorous. The overuse of processed foods has put the phosphorous level much too high, thereby hampering the ideal calcium absorption. High sugar intake also increases calcium excretion. Stress, smoking, alcohol and pollution in the environment are all associated with calcium excretion.

Bone enhancers are moderate exercise using the leg bones, such as walking, hiking, biking and also water drinking, vitamin D from the sunshine, dark leafy greens, and tofu. Vegetarians have stronger and denser bones than people whose diet is predominantly meat. At the age of 70, vegetarian women have greater bone density than carnivores in their 50's.

The milk bubble has been popped! Cow's milk is the perfect food for calves. Breast milk is the perfect food for human infants. You can fulfill your calcium requirements from plant foods. The Chinese have depended on soybean products and leafy greens for good nutrition. American cows get their calcium from the same sources. Why not use these primary sources of calcium rather then second hand from the cow. African nationals and black Americans consume less calcium than most Caucasians, and have less osteoporosis and greater bone density.

More is not necessarily the cure for calcium malabsorption. In studies based on the average American diet, it was found that bone destruction exceeds bone formation for 2 to 5 hours each day. What you assimilate is crucial to bone formation. Pay attention to your intake of animal protein, salt, coffee, sugar, soda pop, processed foods, tobacco, and alcohol. Exercise, drinking adequate water, sunshine, and eating calcium-rich plant foods, are all aids to calcium absorption.

References:
1. Behrstock, Barry, Dr., "A Parents Guide to the Myths and Misconceptions of Child Care," *Family Circle*, Aug. 11, 1981, p. 139.
2. Blum, Sam, "Holy Cow," *New York Times Magazine*, April 6, 1975, pp. 49-50.
3. Brody, Jane, " Personal Health: Breast Feeding," *The New York Times*, March 9,1977.
4. *Consumer Guide,* "Everything You Need To Know About Calcium".
5. *Consumer Reports,* "Milk: Could It Taste Better," June 1982, p. 286.
6. Findlay, Steve, "Brittle Bones", *Nutrition Action,* June 1982, pp. 12-13.
7. Hausman, Patricia, *The Calcium Bible*, Rawson Associates, NY, 1985.
8. Krizmanic, Judy,"News Digest: Bones and Stones," *Vegetarian Times*, September 1988, Issue 133, p.8.
9. Magie, Allan R. "The Real Energy Crisis is a Cow," *Life and Health*, Reprint No. 109.
10. Notelovitz, Morris, MD, *Stand Tall: The Informed Woman's Guide To Preventing Osteoporosis*, Triad Publications, Gainsville, FL, 1982.

Calcium Sources

All measurements are for 1 cup unless otherwise noted.

Collards cooked	289	milligrams
Bok Choy	250	"
Turnip Greens	252	"
Sesame Seeds 2 T	210	"
Kale	210	"
Cows Milk	197	"
Mustard Greens	193	"
Soyagen	190	"
Watercress	189	"
Breast Milk	184	"
Almonds 1/2 cup	160	"
Broccoli	140	"
Broccoli 1 stalk	110	"
Garbanzos cooked	156	"
Black Beans	140	"
Molasses 1 T	137	"
Tofu 4 ounces	130	"
Sunflower Seeds 2 T	124	"
Carob 4 T	120	"
Parsley	120	"
Butternut Squash	82	"
Buckwheat 1 cup cooked	74	"
Soybeans 1/2 cup cooked	66	"
Dates 1/2 cup	50	"
Apricots 1/2 cup	50	"
Figs 2 or 3 small	38	"

Sources:

1. *Sourcebook on Food and Nutrition* Marquis Academic Media.

2. *The New Laurel's Kitchen,* © 1986, published by Ten Speed Press, Berkeley, CA 94707.

BREAKFAST FOODS

Non-Dairy Milks

CASHEW OR ALMOND MILK
Yield: 1 quart

What You Need

1 cup nuts (cashew or
   almonds)
3 cups of water

1 T honey or 1 banana
3 T carob for carob milk

What You Do

1. Begin with 1 cup of nuts and 1 cup of water.
2. Add sweetener and carob to mixture.
3. Blend all ingredients until creamy.
4. Add remaining water until desired consistency.
*Variation: You can add 1/2 t of vanilla or maple flavorings. Add less water and frozen strawberries for a milkshake.

SUNFLOWER-CAROB MILK
Yield: 1 quart

What You Need

1 cup sunflower seeds
3 cups of water
3 T carob

2 bananas or apples
1-2 T honey (if needed)

What You Do

1. Blend smooth 1 cup of the water with the remaining ingredients.
2. Add remaining water.
3. Add your choice of sweetener if needed.

FRUIT AND CAROB MILK
Yield: 1 individual serving

What You Need

1/2 cup sliced apple
1/2 cup sliced banana
 slices

SUNFLOWER-CAROB MILK
coconut or sunflower seeds

What You Do

1. Slice apples and bananas in a individual bowl.
2. Cover fruit with sunflower-carob milk.
3. Sprinkle with coconut or sunflower seeds.

PINA COLADA BREAKFAST MILK
Yield: 3 cups

What You Need

1/2 cup dry coconut
1 cup pineapple chunks

1 cup pineapple juice
2 bananas

What You Do

1. Blend all ingredients in your blender and serve.
2. You can substitute fresh coconut for dry coconut.

STRAWBERRY SMOOTHIE
Yield: 2 1/2 cups

What You Need

2 cups frozen strawberries
1 banana

1/2 cup pineapple or apple
juice

What You Do

1. Place juice and banana in blender.
2. Blend gradually adding frozen strawberries.
*Variation: replace strawberries with frozen peaches.

Introducing Millet

Millet's original roots may be traced to Asia. In ancient and medieval times, millet was the chief grain crop of Europe and parts of Asia. In Europe, millet lost its popularity because it was unsuited for making yeast-raised breads. Today in China, India, Japan, Africa and Eastern Europe, millet continues to be an important food crop. China, India and the Soviet Union lead the world in, the production of millet. In the United States, millet is grown primarily as fodder and silage for animals and birdseed.

Grains called millet, all part of the Grass family, are listed in three different genera. Proso, pearl and foxtail millet are species of the genus panicum. These are the millets grown in the United States for animal feed, hay, birdseed and for human consumption. India has 15 million acres of hybrid proso in cultivation. These species of millet are also the main food of millions in West Africa and South and East Africa. In Nigeria, woman beat out their millet with heavy pestles in hollowed logs. The pounding loosens the chaff, sticks and waste from the seed and then the wind blows all but the yellow seed away. The grain is then ground into a coarse meal, using a stone rolling pin and a stone trough. Nigerians eat millet mixed with water and made into dumplings. They use the dumplings in stew or with spicy gravy. Porridge, ungali, is a popular method of eating millet as well. Travelers will put a little raw meal into their calabash water bottles and then use it as a beverage.

The millet used in Ethiopia is of the Festuca genus of grasses, named teff, and is used in baking bread called injera. This millet is a superior product to millet grown in the United States. Only wheat is superior to teff for its high protein content. Ethiopians eat more millet than any other grain. The northern Chinese attribute their taller stature to their use of millet instead of the white rice which is popular in southern Chinese provinces. (Refer to Mail Order Sources for information on purchasing teff.)

Sorghum, Indian millet, was brought to South Carolina from Africa in the 1700s as food for the slaves. Those slaves with the most strength and endurance during the long and horrible voyage from Africa to the West Indies and the American Colonies were the farmers from agricultural tribes who were accustomed to eating large amounts of whole grains, including millet.

The key to millet's popularity in dry arid land is that it grows well in poor soil and requires less water than most other grains. The yields are large and the growth is rapid. Often Third World farmers will plant millet when drought or disease has caused crop failure. Millet is cold-sensitive, but can withstand high temperatures and low moisture.

Millet is becoming more popular in America today. You can purchase millet in health food stores, and you will be impressed with its unique yellow color and roundness. Millet is soothing to the stomach and therefore a good first food for babies, excellent for ulcer patients, and more easily digested by those allergic to the higher gluten grains. I think you will enjoy the versatility of millet in the recipes that follow.

References:
1.Berry, Erick, *Eating Around the World*, The John Day Co., NY, 1963.
2.Brown, Elizabeth, Grains: *An Illustrated History With Recipes,* Prentice-Hall, Englewood Cliffs, NJ, 1977.
3.DeWit, H.C.D., *Plants of the World*, E.P. Button, NY, 1967, pp. 266-270.
4.Friedman, Emanual ed., Merit Students Encyclopedia, Macmillan, NY, 1981.
5.World Book, Scott Fetzer Co., Chicago, IL, 1984.

MILLET CASSEROLE
Compliments of Linda Warren
Yield: serves 6

What You Need

1 cup millet
4 cups water
3/4 cup raisins
2 cups pineapple juice

2 cups soaked soybeans
3/4 t salt
3/4 cup dried coconut

What You Do

1. Soak 1 cup of soybeans in 3 cups water overnight.
2. Drain and discard water.
3. Blend smooth soybeans and pineapple juice.
4. Mix all ingredients together.
5. Cover and bake at 350° in an oiled casserole for 1 1/2 hours.

OVERNIGHT CROCKPOT MILLET CEREAL
Yield: 4 cups of millet

What You Need

1 cup dry millet
1/2 t salt

4 cups water

What You Do

1. Put dry millet, water, and salt into a crockpot and cover.
2. Set temperature gauge on low and cook overnight 8-10 hours.
3. An easy way to have breakfast ready each morning.
4. Add raisins or dates before serving.

STOVE TOP MILLET CEREAL
Yield: 3-4 cups

What You Need

1 cup millet
1/2 t salt

3-4 cups water

What You Do

1. For moist cereal use 4 cups of water and for a dryer cereal use 3 cups of water.
2. Combine ingredients in covered saucepan. Bring to a boil.
3. Reduce heat. Lightly boil 45-60 minutes.

MILLET STICKS
Yield:16 sticks

What You Need

1 cup dry millet
2 cups water
1/2 t salt
1/4 cup raisins

1/2 cup sunflower seeds
1/2 cup dry, unsweetened coconut
1 cooked medium sweet potato or 1 large banana or 1/2 cup leftover cooked millet

What You Do

1. Choose one of the following: sweet potato, banana, or leftover millet and add to blender.
2. Blend smooth remaining ingredients except raisins.
3. You can make this into patties, but using a cast iron stick pan makes a delicious alternative to bread. You can purchase stick pans in cook stores or hardware stores. Most are cast iron and some have a design of an ear of corn, and some have eleven narrow and smooth sections.
4. Oil stick pans and pour mixture into stick sections.
5. Drop 8 raisins into each section. Cover with existing batter.
6. Bake at 350° for 45-60 minutes. Let cool in pan 5 minutes.
7. Use a smooth edged knife to loosen the sticks. Sticks will dry and harden as they cool.

FINNISH WHIPPED MILLET PUDDING
Yield: serves 4

What You Need

3 cups apple juice
1 1/2 cup ALMOND
CREAM or TOFU WHIPPED
CREAM
1/4 t salt

1 1/2 cups shredded apples
1 cup fresh or frozen
blueberries
1/2 cup dry millet (uncooked)
1/4 cup coconut

What You Do

1. Blend dry millet in your blender to make meal.
2. Bring 3 cups of apple juice plus 1/4 t salt to a boil, turn to low.
3. Immediately with a wire whisk whip the dry millet meal into the juice being careful to avoid lumps.
4. Cover and cook 20 minutes on low.
5. Whip hot cooked millet in a food processor or blender, or beat with an electric beater for 5 minutes.
6. Put in a serving bowl and fold in 1 cup almond or tofu cream and cup shredded apples. Sprinkle with coconut.
7. Chill.
8. Decorate top of pudding with 1/2 cup of remaining cream and blueberries.

*Variation: Serve a pitcher of thick ALMOND or CASHEW MILK to pour over individual servings.

BREAKFAST FOODS

SLIGHTLY NUTTY PUDDING
Reprinted from *NEWSTART Homestyle*
Yield: 4 small servings

What You Need

1/2 cup water
1 cup hot, cooked millet
2 T carob powder
1/8 t salt

1/2 cups dates
2 T peanut butter
1/2 t vanilla
2 T coconut

What You Do

1. Simmer 1/2 cup dates and 1/2 cup water until dates are soft.
2. Blend in blender the dates and water until it becomes creamy.
3. Add carob powder, peanut butter, vanilla, salt and millet and blend.
4. Pour into a serving dish or 4 small pudding cups.
5. Sprinkle top with coconut.
6. Chill and pudding will thicken.

MILLET CHEESE CAKE
Reprinted from *Hartland Heartsavers*
Yield: 8 servings

What You Need

1 1/2 cup pineapple juice
5 cups water
1 1/4 cup uncooked millet
2 T lemon juice

1/3 cup honey
1 T vanilla
1/2 t salt
1/4 cup arrowroot

What You Do

1. Cook millet, salt, and water 45-60 minutes until millet is soft and water is absorbed. Mix all ingredients in a bowl.
2. Blend half of the mixture and pour into a cooking pot. A food processor makes the job easier but a blender will do.
3. Blend the second half and cook all mixture until thickened.
4. Pour into a 9" by 12" baking dish.
5. Top with thickened strawberries or carob frosting. Chill.

MILLET PUDDING
Adapted from *Country Life Natural Foods Cookbook*
Yield: 4 cups

What You Need

2 cups crushed pineapple
1 T vanilla
1 banana

2 cups hot cooked millet
1/2 t salt

What You Do

1. Place a layer of sliced bananas on bottom of an 8"x8" dish.
2. Blend smooth half of remaining ingredients. Pour over banana slices. Repeat process and pour in dish.
3. Sprinkle top with coconut, nuts, raisins, or decorate with sliced kiwi fruit and pomegranate seeds. Chill.
*Variation: Stir in juice of 1 lemon, 1 T grated lemon rind and 2 T honey for LEMON PUDDING.

MILLET FRUIT COOKIES
Yield: 24 cookies

What You Need

1 cup millet flour or millet
2 cups coconut
1/2 t salt
1/2 cup sunflower seeds

3/4 cup pineapple or apple juice
1/2 cup DATE BUTTER
3/4 cup thick applesauce
1 large ripe banana

What You Do

1. Blend 1 cup dry millet in blender to make millet flour or you can buy commercial millet flour at a Health Food Store.
2. Blend sunflower seeds in blender. Mix all ingredients.
3. Drop by teaspoons on oiled pan. Bake at 350° for 20 min. Check bottoms for browness. Reduce to 250° for 10 min.
4. Let cool on pan, they will become firm. Refrigerate leftovers.
*Variation: For a sweeter cookie add 1/4 cup barley malt or honey and reduce juice by 1/4 cup. May add 1/2 c. carob chips, walnuts or raisins to batter. Substitute rice flour for millet.

MILLET FLAT BREAD
Yield: 1 cookie sheet full

What You Need

Dry ingredients:
1 cup millet flour
1/2 cup unsweetened coconut
1/2 t ground anise
2 t ground coriander
1/2 t salt

Wet ingredients:
2 T sweetener
1 cup water
1 cup tofu
1 cooked sweet potato
1 T oil (optional)

What You Do

1. Mix dry ingredients. Blend smooth remaining ingredients.
2. Mix all ingredients. Spread on oiled cookie sheet.
3. Bake at 350° for 45-60 minutes. Cut into squares. Serve.
* Suggestion: Commercial fine millet flour can be purchased in a natural food store and makes a lighter bread. You can blend a cup of millet in the blender to make a coarse flour.

MILLET PUDDING CAKE
Yield: 8" by 8" baking dish

What You Need

1 1/2 cup prunes
1/2 cup orange juice or
   pineapple juice
2 cups water

4 cups of leftover MILLET
   STICKS, MILLET
   FLATBREAD or
   BUCKWHEAT WAFFLES

What You Do

1. Simmer prunes and water until prunes soften then let cool.
2. Blend prunes in a blender to make prune butter.
3. Crumble leftover material in a baking dish. Top with juice.
4. Spread generously with prune butter.
5. You can make a second layer and spread prune butter on top.
    The more prune butter you use the more moist it will be.
6. Bake at 350° for 20 minutes. Top with ALMOND CREAM.
7. Serve for breakfast or as a dessert.

MILLET WAFFLES
Yield 2-8" Waffles

What You Need

2 cups dry millet
2 cups water

1/2 cup dry garbanzo beans
1/2 t salt

What You Do

1. Soak beans 6-8 hours in 3 cups of water.
2. Drain beans and discard water.
3. Blend smooth the beans, water, millet and salt.
4. Bake in oiled waffle iron 10-15 minutes.

APPLE FRITTERS

What You Need

2 cups water
1 cup dry millet
1/2 cup coconut

1/2 cup sunflower seeds
1/4 t salt
apples

What You Do

1. Blend smooth all but apples.
2. Peel, core and slice apples in 1/2 inch rings.
3. Dip apples in batter. Place on oiled cookie sheet.
4. Bake at 350° for 15 minutes on each side or until light brown.

BREADS AND SPREADS

Breads and Spreads

BREADS AND SPREADS

Eat a Whole Thing

Variety is one **Key** which opens the door to more healthful and interesting meals. We are all familiar with wheat, oats and rice, but have you used whole rye or flaked barley or perhaps raw buckwheat groats lately? Have you ever heard of millet for human consumption? Those small light yellow millet kernels in wild bird seed are a powerhouse of nutrition for humans as well.

Interestingly enough, Americans have a high propensity to wheat allergies, South Americans to corn allergies, Chinese to rice allergies, and Japanese to soy allergies. Yes, the connection is overuse. The more we eat one type of food to the exclusion of other foods, we open ourselves to an allergic response, and even to addiction.

Rotation is another **Key** to opening the door to better health. You can substitute flaked barley or rye cereal for traditional cooked oatmeal. Add grated apples and raisins to help the taste buds adjust to a new taste. If you are serving corn on the cob, add corn bread, corn crackers, or popcorn instead of wheat bread. You get variety in texture, and at the same time you are able to keep your meal simple. If you have an allergic reaction to wheat, you may be able to tolerate wheat on a four day rotation. You can use raw buckwheat groats, found in health food stores, instead of roasted buckwheat, and the flavor is much more mild. Give your taste buds the challenge of the hearty tastes of a variety of whole grains.

Wholeness is a third **Key** to opening the door to optimum well-being. Longer storage time, easier mixing, and greater consumer acceptability have made white flour a big seller, but you are short-changed in health. Store-bought bread, even whole wheat types, lacks the crustiness that reminds us to chew well and stimulate our gums. Eat your grains whole rather than processed, bleached, bolted, enriched, ballooned, and preserved. The main excuse for not baking your own bread is time. Remember the proverb: we reap what we sow. Diverticulitis, spastic colon, and diabetes are directly related to the over-use of refined products. The time invested in baking bread is well spent, instead of waiting in a physician's office to counsel on ways to deal with disease. The harvest reaped from eating refined foods doesn't occur immediately. The consumer needs to reason from cause to effect to realize that good eating habits now will pay off in good health in the future.

BREADS AND SPREADS

In his book *Everything You Wanted to Know About Nutrition,* Dr. David Ruben notes that the average American eats 6 to 8 grams of fiber a day. Vegetarians from America eat 24 grams, as do rural South African Bantus. The Bantu diet consist or cornmeal, bananas, potatoes, and beans. The average American may develop diabetes, ulcers, colon diseases, high blood pressure, heart attacks or cancer. These diseases are nearly-nonexistent among the Bantu peoples and significantly less with American vegetarians. Stress, cigarette smoking, alcohol, and job and environment-related pollution also effects human disease. Fiber is not the only answer. Adding 4 tablespoons of bran to an otherwise poor diet will not necessarily produce healthful results. Eating whole grains, beans, seeds, and fresh fruit and vegetables is the best guarantee for adequate fiber. Eat the whole food. Eat a variety of foods and rotate your choices, and you will begin to enjoy optimum health.

CIRCLE OF NUTRITION CRACKER TRAY

Make several types of crackers and encircle the tray, leaving the center open for samples of fruit and nut butters for cracker-dipping.

RYE-OAT CRACKERS WITH CHEESY TASTE
Yield: 1 cookie sheet

What You Need

3 cups oats
2 cups rye, barley, or
   buckwheat flour
1 cup yeast flakes

1/2 t salt
1/2 cup oil
1 cup water

What You Do

1. Mix grains and salt.
2. Add oil and mix well.
3. Add water gradually to get ball of dough. Add additional water if needed.
4. Divide in half. Spread each half on 11 x 15 cookie sheet. No greasing is necessary.
5. Place wax paper on top of dough and roll out with sturdy glass or small rolling pin.
6. Score in desired size.
7. Bake at 250° for 1 hour or until dry.

MILLET OR BUCKWHEAT CRACKERS
Yield: 2 cookie sheets full

What You Need

1 cup dry millet or buckwheat groats	1/2 cup sunflower, sesame or pumpkin seeds
1/2 cup unsweetened coconut	1/4 t salt
	2 cups water

What You Do

1. Put all ingredients in blender and blend till creamy. You may need to add more water. Desired consistency like pancake batter.
2. Pour out thinly on oiled cookie sheets or in cast iron corn stick pans.
3. Bake at 300° for 20 minutes; then remove from oven and score to desired size.
4. Replace in oven at 300° for another 25 minutes and let crisp at 250° till done.

*Variation: Add ripe banana or 2 T sweetener or 1/4 cup applesauce or 1 t coriander and 1/2 t anise.

CORN CRACKERS
Reprinted from *Nature's Banquet* by Living Springs
Yield: 4 dozen crackers

What You Need

1 1/4 cup water	1 t salt
1 T coconut	1 cup cornmeal
1 1/2 T sesame seeds	1/4 cup oats, dry
1/4 cup cashew nuts	

What You Do

1. Blend smooth all but cornmeal; then stir in cornmeal.
2. Spread on 2 oiled cookie sheets. Bake at 350° for 20 minutes.
3. Remove from oven and score with a knife.
4. Reduce heat to 300° and bake for 10-20 minutes longer until crackers will lift off the cookie sheets.

BREADS AND SPREADS

BASIC GARBANZO CRACKERS
Yield: 2 cookie sheets

What You Need

1 cup soaked garbanzos
3/4 cup sunflower seeds
1/4 t salt

3/4 cup dried coconut
2 1/4 cups water

What You Do

1. Soak 1/2 cup garbanzos in 1 1/2 cups of water overnight.
2. Drain and rinse and discard water.
3. Preheat oven to 300°.
4. Blend above ingredients to make a pourable pancake-like batter. Add more water if needed.
5. Oil two non stick 11 x 15 cookie sheets and divide batter between the two sheets.
6. Sprinkle tops with sesame seeds, poppy seeds, or flaked seaweed.
7. Place in oven for 15 minutes, then remove and score with a plastic knife into desired size. Return to oven.
8. Lower oven to 200° and bake 1 hour or until dry and crisp.
*Variations: Use 2 T onion powder and 1/2 t garlic powder for zesty taste. Use 3-4 T yeast flakes for cheesy flavor. Use soybeans instead instead of garbanzo beans.

*   If you don't have non stick cookie sheets, add to blender:

2 T tahini   1 T arrowroot

Use well oiled cookie sheets.

CORN CHIPS
Reprinted from *Cooking With Natural Foods*
Yield: 1 cookie sheet

What You Need

1 1/2 cups fine cornmeal
little salt
1/2 cup almonds ground fine

1 cup water
1/2 t vanilla

What You Do

1. Blend ingredients and let stand a few minutes.
2. Blend again, batter should be thin.
3. Drop in circles on a non-stick cookie sheet.
4. Bake 5-10 minutes in a 350° oven.
5. Should be light brown and crisp.

Flat Breads

SOY-CORN BREAD
Yield: 2 cookie sheets

What You Need

1 cup soaked soybeans
1/4 cup dried coconut
1/2 t salt
1 cup cornmeal

3 T tahini or nut butter
1/2 cup raisins
2 cups liquid- possible
   combinations: apple juice,
   water, or applesauce

What You Do

1. Soak 1/2 cup dry soybeans in 1 1/2 cups water overnight or 8 hours.
2. Drain and rinse.
3. Blend smooth: beans, tahini, salt.
4. Stir in cornmeal and raisins.
5. Oil two 11 x 15 cookie sheets.
6. Spoon out by tablespoons onto sheets.
7. Bake at 350° for 20-30 minutes.

BUCKWHEAT BREAD
Yield:1 cookie sheet

What You Need

5 cups water
pinch of salt

1 cup Cream of Buckwheat

What You Do

1. Place ingredients in crockpot overnight on low setting.
2. Pour onto 11 x 15 cookie sheet. Refrigerate until solid. Cut into squares.
3. Bake on oiled cookie sheet or fry on lightly oiled Teflon or Silverstone griddle.
4. Serve with favorite spread.

BARLEY FLAT BREAD
Yield: 4 servings

What You Need

1 cup barley flour
1/2 cup sesame seed meal
1 t oil

1/4 cup cold water
1/4 t salt
1/4 cup finely minced onion

What You Do

1. Blend dry sesame seeds to meal in blender.
2. Mix flour, sesame seeds, salt, and onions in a bowl.
3. Add oil and mix.
4. Stir in water a little at a time until dough holds together.
5. Divide into 4 balls.
6. Roll out 1/4 inch thick between wax paper.
7. Bake at 400° in oven for 15 minutes on lightly oiled cookie sheet.

BREADS AND SPREADS

ITALIAN CORNMEAL POLENTA
Yield: 16 squares

What You Need

3 cups water
1/2 t salt

1 cup cornmeal

What You Do

1. Mix in a saucepan water, cornmeal and salt.
2. Bring to boil, stirring with wire whip to keep fromlumping.
3. Lower heat and simmer 1 hour.
4. Turn into lightly oiled glass 9 x 9 x 2 loaf pan.
5. Chill in refrigerator 3 to 4 hours.
6. Preheat oven to 375°.
7. Cut polenta into 16 squares.
8. Arrange on an oiled cookie sheet and place in oven.
9. Allow 15 minutes for each side.
*Serving suggestions:
1. For fruit polenta, add 1/2 cup raisins to step 3, and, after step 9, remove and serve with applesauce topping or fruit jams.
2. For cheese polenta, after step 8, grate soy cheese and sprinkle on squares. Bake 15 minutes or until cheese melts. Serve immediately. May top with tomato sauce.

SURPRISE BALLS OR MIX AND MATCH PATTIES

Any amount of leftover cereal. Good combinations are cornmeal, oats and millet. Barley and rye cereal make patties ooze, so use less of these grains in combinations. Place balls on oiled cookie sheet. Bake at 350° for 15 minutes. Turn or role over and let bake for another 15 minutes. For patties: use canning jar rings as molds, form patties on oiled cookie sheet, and bake as with balls. You can add raisins, dates or sweetener, and they become yummy as cookies.

BARLEY-OAT MUFFINS

Reprinted from *Nature's Banquet* by Living Springs
Yield: 6 muffins

What You Need

1 cup rolled oats
1/2 cup raisins
3/4 cup water
2 T oil

1 cup barley flour or flaked
  barley blended in blender
1 cup shredded apples
1/2 t salt

What You Do

1. Combine barley flour, rolled oats and raisins.
2. Separately combine water, apples, oil, salt, and mix well.
3. Combine wet ingredients with dry and let stand 10-15 minutes.
4. Spoon into greased muffin pans, forming rounded muffins.
5. Bake at 350° for 25-30 minutes until browned.
6. These muffins will be dense, but delicious and filling.

DATE NUT BREAD

Reprinted from *The Country Life Natural Foods Cookbook*
Yield: 1 small loaf

What You Need

1/3 cup DATE BUTTER
1 t vanilla
cups chopped dates
2 cups chopped walnuts

1/3 to 1/2 cup orange juice
1 cup whole wheat flour or   chopped 2 2 2
            rice flour

What You Do

1. Mix all ingredients well.
2. Spoon into small, oiled loaf pan.
3. Bake at 300° for 45 to 50 minutes, but don't let the bread get too dry.
4. Let cool and then slice thin.

Yeast Breads

BANANA RYE BREAD
Yield: 2 loaves

What You Need

2 T active dry yeast
6 cups rye flour
3 T oil
3 cups ripe bananas
  mashed (about 6)

1 cup warm water
1 T salt
2 T sweetener

What You Do

1. Dissolve yeast in warm water with sweetener in large mixing bowl.
2. In another bowl, mix together 3 cups rye flour and all the rest of the ingredients.
3. Spoon into yeast water and mix well, gradually adding, stirring in the rest of the flour.
4. Mix until smooth, knead on rye floured board 10 minutes. Be sure it isn't sticky.
5. Place on greased bowl, turn once and cover. Let rise 2 hours.
6. Turn out on floured board and knead 3 minutes. Mold into loaves (2) and place in greased pans or as circles on cookie sheet. Cover with damp cloth.
7. Let rise 1 hour.
8. Bake at 425° for 12 minutes, lower to 350° and bake 45 minutes.
9. Remove bread and set out to cool.

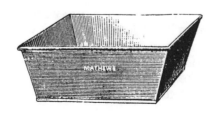

BROWN RICE FLOUR MUFFINS
Yield: 12 small muffins or 1 loaf

What You Need

3 cups brown rice flour
   or buckwheat flour
1/2 t salt
2 T honey

2 T oil
1 T active dry yeast
1 1/2 cups warm water
1/2 cup raisins or dates
   (optional)

What You Do

1. Dissolve yeast in water and honey.
2. When yeast bubbles, add the rest of the ingredients. Mix well and add more warm water (minimal) to make mixture soft, but not runny.
3. Place in greased muffin tins, filling 3/4's full.
4. Let stand 1/2 hour.
5. Bake in oven at 350° for 30 minutes or until top browns or cracks.

RICE BREAD
Reprinted from *Uprisings: The Whole Grain Bakers Book*
Yield: 2 loaves

What You Need

2 1/2 cups warm water
2 cups rice flour
1/4 cup rolled oats
1 T dry yeast
1/2 t salt

1/2 cup sunflower seeds
1/2 cup millet flour
1/4 cup soy flour
1 T sweetener

What You Do

1. Dissolve yeast in a bowl with warm water and sweetener.
2. Add all remaining ingredients and beat well.
3. Batter should be soupy.
4. Pour into well greased bread pans and let rise uncovered 20 to 30 minutes. Bake at 375° for 1 hour.
5. Cool 5 minutes in pans then turn on rack for further cooling.

Jams

DATE BUTTER

Reprinted from *The Country Life Natural Foods Cookbook*
Yield: 2 cups

What You Need

1 cup dates   1 cup water

What You Do

1. Chop dates.
2. Simmer dates and water until soft.
3. Cool and blend in blender or mash with fork.
4. Store in refrigerator (freezable).
5. Use as spread or in cooking instead of sugar or honey.
*Variations: Use 1 cup prunes and 1 cup water, or 1 cup raisins and 1/2 cup water, instead of dates.

APRICOT MARMALADE

Reprinted from *The Country Life Natural Foods Cookbook*
Yield: 3 1/2 cups marmalade

What You Need

1/2 cup dates   2 cups pineapple juice or
1 cup apricots   water

What You Do

1. Soak dates, apricots and juice overnight, and blend in blender.
2. Or if you are in a hurry: simmer ingredients 5 minutes, cool and blend in blender.
3. Delicious replacement for jam.

BREADS AND SPREADS

REFRIGERATOR FRUIT JAM
Organic Gardening, Rodale Press, August 1981
Yield:2 pints

What You Need

4 cups fresh fruit - peaches or strawberries
3/4 cup apple juice concentrate
3 T Emes gelatin or 2 t agar powder

What You Do

1. In a saucepan heat to boiling, stirring constantly: 6 oz. apple juice concentrate and gelatin.
2. Turn down to simmer and add fresh fruit.
3. Smash fruit to consistency you prefer. A potato masher works well.
4. Simmer 30 minutes then cool.
5. Store in jars and place in refrigerator.
6. Jam will thicken after several hours in refrigerator.

FIG APPLE JAM
Yield: 4 cups jam

What You Need

3 cups black mission figs
1 1/2 cups dried apples
orange peels from 1 orange
4 cups of water

What You Do

1. Simmer all ingredients 40 minutes.
2. Cool and then blend in blender to make thick jam.

BREADS AND SPREADS

WHIPPED TAHINI
Yield: 1/4 cup

What You Need

1/4 cup tahini   2 T water

What You Do

1. Add water to tahini and whip with spoon until white and creamy. You can add more water, if necessary.

TAHINI-CAROB SPREAD
Yield: 1/2 cup

What You Need

1/4 cup tahini   3-4 T water
2 T carob powder   2-4 T sunflower seeds

What You Do

1. Mix all but sunflower seeds by spoon until creamy.
2. Prepare seeds by lightly roasting them in a frying pan over medium heat stirring constantly. Seeds are done when they start to pop and turn darker. Keep a constant watch.
3. Add sunflower seeds and mix in.
4. Spread is good on bread, crackers, waffles, bananas or apples.

FIG PINEAPPLE JAM
Yield: 1 1/2 cups

What You Need

1 cup Turkish figs   1 cup pineapple juice

What You Do

1. Simmer figs and juice in a pot until soft.
2. Let cool then blend.
3. Delicious spread on waffles or crackers.

SESAME SPREAD
Yield: 1 cup

What You Need

1/2 cup sesame seeds
1/4 t salt

1/2 cup hot water
4-6 T DATE BUTTER

What You Do

1. Grind sesame seeds in a dry blender to make meal.
2. Pour the ground seeds back into the measuring cup.
3. Place hot water, salt, and date butter in blender.
4. Blend ingredients at low speed.
5. As blender turns, add sesame seeds 1 tablespoon at a time until the mixture thickens.
6. Turn blender to high speed for 10 seconds to insure a good blend.
7. Serve immediately or chill.
8. Use as a spread for crackers, sticks, flatbread, or pancakes.
*Variation: Add 1 T vanilla or 2 T carob.

MILLET BUTTER
Compliments of *Leslie Caza*
Yield: 1/2 cup butter

What You Need

1/4 cup millet
1 T unflavored Emes
   Kosher Gel
1/2 t imitation butter flavor

3/4 cup water
1 1/2 cups water
1 t salt

What You Do

1. Lightly boil millet and 3/4 c. water in covered pan 60 minutes.
2. Place 1 1/2 c. water and Emes in pan. Let sit 5 minutes.
3. Now bring gel to boil and turn heat off, stirring to prevent sticking, and allow to cool.
4. Blend cooked millet and Emes gel and seasonings.
5. Pour into 1/2 pint containers. Chill.
6. The butter will keep about 10 days.

MILLET COCO BUTTER
Yield: 2 1/2 cups butter

What You Need

1/2 cup cooked hot
  millet or cornmeal
1/2 cup coconut

1/4 cup water
2 small cooked carrots
1/4 t salt

What You Do

1. Put all ingredients in blender and blend, adding enough water to allow blender to spin.
2. Blend until smooth.
3. Put in glass container and refrigerate.
4. Mix will solidify when fully cooled.

Grains That Are Not Grains

Buckwheat, amaranth and quinoa (pronounced "keen-wa") are not members of the Graminea family of cereal grains, such as wheat, rye, oats, barley or millet. They are botanically classified as dry fruits or annual herbs, possessing good taste and milling characteristics.

Buckwheat, with its three-cornered seed, is related to the rhubarb plant and part of the Polyonceae family. Amaranth and its wild relative, pigweed, are in the Amaranthus family, while quinoa is in the Chenopodium family along with lamb's-quarters. All four families are classified together with the flowering plants, Angiospermae, which is a subclass of monocotyledonea.

Amaranth, quinoa or buckwheat might prove to be a blessing to those with gluten allergies or intolerance to the traditional mucous-producing grains. Amaranth, a broad leaf plant, was cultivated by the Aztecs and used for its high protein "cereal" seed and greens. The Aztecs used amaranth in their religious ceremonies, so consequently the Spanish conquistadors suppressed its cultivation and introduced and developed corn as a main crop.

Amaranth grows in semi-arid environments and has successfully been introduced in India and Nepal. It has potentially high yields, but mechanical harvesting recovers only 50% of the actual yield due to the tiny mustard-sized seed. As a valuable source of protein,

Quinoa

Amaranth has high levels of lysine, which cereal grains are low in. Being low in gluten, and high in calcium and iron, makes Amaranth a choice worth experimenting with. Amaranth is used in unleavened breads rather than yeast-raised breads, as well as pancakes, crackers and cookies.

Quinoa (pronounced "keen-wa"), a good source of protein, calcium, iron and B-vitamins, was the main staple for South American Andes Incas, and today is grown and used in the highlands of Bolivia, Chili, Ecuador, and Peru by Aymara and Quechua Indians. Like Amaranth, with 16% protein, the amino acid balance of quinoa excels cereal grains and is more similar to the protein balance of soybeans.

According to a Texas A&M University report, quinoa, an oil seed, has small starch granules and strong tenacity between the starch granules, which give it the binding quality that traditional cereal grains have.

Like Amaranth, quinoa plants produce a small seed, but have a lower yield. The seeds are covered with saponin, a bitter resin-like substance, and when rinsed make a soapy solution in water. You must rinse the seeds before use. Researchers are attempting to develop a saponin-free strain, but ecologists recognize the bitter tasting saponin as a natural insecticide. The bitter taste prevents insect and bird predation. The recommendation is for the consumer to wash off the saponin rather than have the farmer rely on insecticides.

Quinoa thrives in high altitudes and with low rainfall and poor soil conditions. Quinoa Corporation in Boulder, Colorado, has been importing the seed from South America and growing it in the San Luis Valley of the Colorado Rockies since the early 1980s. The seed is versatile in its uses as a cooked cereal like rice, flour for pancakes, and cookies. The leaves can be eaten as vegetables or used for animal fodder, the stalks burned for fuel, and saponin rinse water used as a shampoo. Even though quinoa and amaranth are expensive, their low gluten quality is a plus for a person with grain allergies.

Buckwheat is more reasonably priced, and raw buckwheat has a mild flavor that can be used in making waffles and pancakes, and it is a source for Japanese sorba and Korean 100% buckwheat noodles. Buckwheat is 13% protein,is rich in iron and B-vitamins, and provides 2% of the daily calcium requirement. You can also sprout the unhulled black seed, or grow buckwheat grass, which is rich in rutin, a bioflavonoid believed to contribute to building and maintaining strong capillaries. Buckwheat is extremely hardy and almost blight-free, which makes it one of the few commercially grown crops that has no need of pesticides, or herbicides.

Buckwheat, quinoa and amaranth are whole foods with high quality nutrition and fiber, and because they are grown without chemicals, are a choice worth investigating.

References:
1. Arrowhead Mills, Inc., Lab Report, No. 5298, Quinoa and Amaranth, O'Neal Scientific Services, December 1985.
2. Birkett Mills, *A History of Buckwheat*, a pamphlet. National Buckwheat Institute, P.O. Box 440, Penn Yan, NY 14527.
3. Bourne, Malcom, Professor of Food Science and Technology, Cornell University, Correspondence May 3, 1988 and June 29,1988.
4. Delicious Pantry, "Discovering Quinoa", *Delicious*, Nov.-Dec. 1986, pp.50-51.
5. Fabricant, Florence, "An Andean Legacy: Quinoa," *The New York Times,* Feb. 12, 1986, p. 25.
6. Johnson, L.A., Dr., "Processing Varieties of Oilseeds: Lupine and Quinoa", *Report to Natural Fibers and Foods Commission of Texas*, 1979-80, Texas A&M University.
7. National Buckwheat Institute, "Buckwheat Backgrounder," a pamphlet. National Buckwheat Institute.
8. Rodale Research Center, *Protein and Amino Acid Contents of the Grain Amaranth*, pp. 1-5.
9. Sokolov, Raymond, "The Good Seed," *Natural History,* April 1986, pp. 102-105.
10. Tucker, Jonathan, "Amaranth: The Once and Future Crop," *Bio Science,* Vol. 36, No. 1, Jan. 1986, pp.9-13.
11. Wood, Rebecca, "Tale of a Food Survivor, Quinoa," *East-West Journal,* April 1985, pp. 64-68.

AMARANTH TOFU CRACKERS
Yield: 36 crackers

What You Need

3/4 cup amaranth or rinsed quinoa	1/3 cup sunflower seeds
	1/3 cup coconut
1/4 lb. tofu	1/2 t salt
2 T sweetener	3 cups water

What You Do

1. Blend all ingredients in blender to make a pourable batter.
2. Pour out on 2 well oiled cookie sheets.
3. Bake at 300° for 15 minutes.
4. Take out of oven and score into squares.
5. Turn oven to 200°, continue baking until crisp, about 1 hour.

AMARANTH PANCAKES
Yield: serves 3

What You Need

1 cup cooked amaranth	1/2 cup coconut
1/2 cup sunflower seeds	1/4 lb. tofu
2 T tahini	2 T sweetener

What You Do

1. Blend all ingredients in your blender to make pourable pancake batter.
2. Cook on an oiled Silverstone or Teflon griddle at medium heat.
*Variation: Rinse 1 cup quinoa seeds several times and substitute for cooked amaranth.

BREADS AND SPREADS

AMARANTH MACAROONS
Yield: 1 dozen

What You Need

2 ripe bananas
2 cups coconut
1/2 cup apple juice concentrate
1/2 lb. tofu

1 cup amaranth or quinoa flour
1/3 cup cashew butter
1/2 cup raisins or carob
chips or chopped nuts

What You Do

1. Mash bananas with a fork.
2. Add flour and coconut to mashed bananas.
3. Blend smooth cashew butter, juice and tofu.
4. Mix well all ingredients and spoon by tablespoons on oiled cookie sheet.
5. Bake at 350° for 12 to 20 minutes or until bottoms brown slightly.

AMARANTH PIE CRUST
Yield: one 9 inch pie crust

What You Need

1 cup amaranth flour
1/2 cup coconut

1/2 almond butter
1/2 cup water

What You Do

1. In a mixing bowl mix flour and coconut.
2. Add 1/2 cup almond butter and mix thoroughly.
3. Add 1/2 cup water and mix into a ball.
4. Let rest 10 minutes.
5. Roll out between wax paper.
6. Oil top rim of pie plate for pre-baked pie shell.
7. Bake 15 to 20 minutes at 350°.

Oiling Cooking Surfaces

Your state of health is a good determiner of how much free fats in the form of oil you can tolerate. If you have health problems like obesity, high blood pressure and diabetes, and are on a special remedial diet, then you should be careful of your total free fat use. People in good health should still only use free fats sparingly. Following are a variety of alternatives that prevent foods from sticking to cooking surfaces.

1. Lightly oil cookie sheets with olive oil or another polyunsaturated oil. The best oil to use is olive oil. After you oil your cookie sheet or bread pan, drain off any excess back into your oil jar. I keep a special jar especially for oiling cooking surfaces. Because I use free fats sparingly in my cooking, if at all, I don't feel it is detrimental to use a little oil in coating cooking surfaces. Just remember how concentrated oil is. For example, it takes 12 ears of corn to make 1 tablespoon of corn oil.

2. Silverstone and Teflon cookware usually only have to be oiled once. I have a Teflon-covered waffle iron; I oil the first time, and make up to nine waffles without having to oil the iron again. I also have a Silverstone griddle which I use for tofu pancakes, and I can oil it once and use it through two recipes of pancakes without oiling again.

3. "Pam" spray is a lecithin-based spray and is readily available in grocery stores. Lecithin is one of the end products of soy oil. Purchase liquid lecithin in the vitamin section of your natural foods store. Usually it is sold in a narrow mouthed jar. It is best to transfer it to a wide-mouthed jar by heating it in hot water and pouring it into the wide-mouthed jar. Store it in your refrigerator. Apply by dotting 1/4 to 1/2 teaspoon portions over a cookie sheet and spread with your hand or paper towel. Use paper toweling to wipe off your hands, as liquid lecithin is difficult, if not impossible, to remove from cloth. Lecithin will foam, so be careful to watch for overbrowning when cooking with it.

4. For oil-less cooking you can purchase Parchment Paper or Reusable Line N Bake from a specialty store selling kitchen equipment and cooking aids. Parchment Paper is a non-stick pan liner and Line N Bake is a flexible reusable sheet of Teflon guaranteed for one year. Foil baking cups are oil-less linings for muffins and are readily available in grocery stores.

5. The use of cornmeal on a cookie sheet will keep French bread or round loaves from sticking. Watch for over-browning on the bottom of the loaf.

MAIN DISHES AND GRAVIES

Main Dishes and Gravies

MAIN DISHES AND GRAVIES

Disease in Animals

God's original diet for man did not include animals as food. Not until after the flood, when every green thing on the earth had been destroyed, did man receive permission to eat the flesh of animals. With this permission came careful restrictions. Unclean and clean animals were distinguished, and the consuming of fat and blood was strictly forbidden.

Flesh has never been the best food, but its use today is doubly objectionable because of the disease in animals. Shellfish is a whole food that is served complete with its intestinal tract along with its feces. Shellfish feed on raw sewage in polluted waters. They are filter feeders that suck in large amounts of water and filter out all microorganisms in the water.

Many of these organisms are disease-causing and are very concentrated in shellfish. Oysters have been found to have concentrated polio virus from 20 to 60 times the level found in the surrounding sea water. The July 1972 issue of *Prevention* magazine describes the shellfish as dirty and dangerous for human consumption. God gave unclean animals the job of scavengers, not the job of a good food source for man.

Even clean animals can be unsafe to eat today. In the February 18,1974 issue of *Newsweek*, the connection between beef eating and bowel cancer is discussed. The highest percentage of bowel cancer is in Scotland where beef cattle are raised as a prime industry. In a 2 pound charcoal-broiled steak there is as much benzopyrene as in 600 cigarettes. The fat from the steak dropping on the charcoal makes a toxic smoke which penetrates the meat. The April 3, 1964 issue of *Time* reports on a woman research scientist who contracted the very same strain of leukemia that her experimental chickens had. Animal disease can be transferred to humans.

You don't have to depend on animal food as your source of protein. All the essential amino acids that make up protein can be found in natural whole foods. Grains, vegetables, fruits, beans, and nuts vary in their levels of the various amino acids. By combining beans and grains or nuts and grains, comparable and ample protein is achieved. Variety is the key to getting proper nutrition out of your foods.

In her book *Future Foods*, Barbara Ford explains that you can feed 14 times as many people from land which grows crops to feed people instead of land which grows crops to feed animals to feed people. Meat is high in cholesterol and fat and devoid of fiber. Red meats contain 14 grams of uric acid per pound. Uric

140

acid has a similar chemical structure to caffeine, and gives a similar effect of stimulating and then depressing, according to an article in *Time* magazine, September 10, 1979, called "Drugged Cow: Feed for Thought."

Physical endurance is sustained from eating foods rich in carbohydrates and not protein. Teddy Roosevelt said that "if you hitch a lion (meat eater) to a plow he will fall from exhaustion after 1 or 2 times across the field, but the horse (vegetarian) can plow that field all day." A team of athletes were given 3 standard bicycle endurance tests. On a high fat, high protein diet, the men cycled 57 minutes to exhaustion. On a mixed diet of meat, vegetables and grain, they endured 1 hour and 54 minutes. A high carbohydrate diet allowed the athletes to endure 2 hours and 47 minutes showing that carbohydrates and not protein gives humans the staying power to endure.

More than 10 million Americans are vegetarians, according to Jane Brody in the October 12, 1983, *New York Times*. Millions of additional Americans are eating less meat and poultry. Why is this? Heart disease, high blood pressure, cancer, and obesity and its complications afflict meat eaters at a significantly higher rate than vegetarians. Vegetarians who eat whole grains, beans, dark leafy greens, fruits, nuts, and seeds will obtain the necessary protein, calcium, and iron that meat supplies in the meat eaters diet.

Plant food is lower in cost, calories, disease, fat, cholesterol, drugs and chemicals, and filth, but high in endurance energy. Animal food is high in cost, calories, disease, fat, cholesterol, drugs and chemicals, and filth, and low in endurance energy. Why don't you seriously weigh these pros and cons?

References:
1. Akers, Keith, *The Vegetarian Activist*, "Bad News for Chicken and Fish Eaters", Vol. 1, No. 1, March 1983, p. 3.
2. Astrand, Per Olaf, *Nutrition Today*, "Something Old and Something New", June 1968, pp. 9-11.
3. Davis, Thomas, *Your Life and Health*, "The National Research Council Says: Reduce Cancer Risk Through Diet", Vol. 97, No. 10, Oct. 1982, p. 4.
4. *Nutrition Reviews*, 25: No. 1, Jan. 1967, pp 8-9.
5. Parret, Owen, MD, *Diseases of Food Animals*, Southern Publishing Association, Nashville, TN, 1939.
6. Scharffenberg, John, MD, *Problems with Meat*, Woodbridge Press, Santa Barbara, CA 93111, 1979.
7. Schell Orville, *Modern Meat*, Random House, 1984.
8. Thrash, Agatha, MD, and Thrash, Calvin, MD, *The Animal Connection*, New Lifestyle Books, Seale, AL, 1983.

MAIN DISHES AND GRAVIES

Main Dishes

CHICK PEA A LA KING

Adapted from *The Country Life Natural Foods Cookbook*
Yield: serves 5

What You Need

2 T olive oil
2 T water
1/2 cup cashew pieces
2 T HOMESTYLE CHICKEN
   SEASONING
2 large pimentos, diced
2-3 cups cooked garbanzo beans

1/2 cup onion, chopped
2 cups water
4 t sesame seeds
1/2 t salt
1 T potato starch
1 1/2 cup green peas

What You Do

1. Saute onion, chopped, with olive oil and water.
2. Blend until smooth: water, cashew pieces, sesame seeds, chicken style seasoning, salt, and potato starch.
3. Add blended sauce to sauteed onions; then add green peas, large pimentos, diced, and cooked garbanzos.
4. Cook until thickened, stirring. Serve over rice or noodles.
*Variation: In dish place 3 cups of cooked mung bean thread, then add CHICKPEA A LA KING and bake 20 minutes at 350°.

HOMESTYLE CHICKEN SEASONING

Reprinted from *The Country Life Natural Foods Cookbook*
Yield: 1 1/2 - 2 cups

What You Need

21 T yeast flakes
3 1/2 t salt
2 1/2 t celery seed, ground
2 1/2 t garlic powder
1 1/4 t paprika
1/2 t turmeric

2 1/2 t sweet pepper flakes, opt
3 t onion powder
2 1/2 t thyme
1 1/4 t marjoram
1 1/4 t rosemary
1 t parsley

1. Blend all together.
A sweet, nonirritating herb seasoning.

MAIN DISHES AND GRAVIES

GARBANZO - BROCCOLI SKILLET DINNER
Yield: serves 4-6

What You Need

2 cups cooked garbanzos
1 1/2 heads broccoli
3 cloves garlic minced
onion powder, garlic powder and salt to taste

1 large onion
1 handful fresh parsley
1/2 cup water

What You Do

1. Slice large onion into rings.
2. Steam onion rings and in water.
3. Separate broccoli flowers from stems. Peel stems, slice medium thin, and add to onions.
4. Steam for about 5 minutes.
5. Add parsley garbanzos. Mix and steam until broccoli is cooked through.
6. Season with onion powder, garlic powder and salt to taste, or just enjoy the natural vegetable combination.
7. Serve over brown rice or mung bean thread.

SAVORY BAKED GARBANZOS
Adapted from *The Vegetarian Epicure* by Anna Thomas
Yield: 4 cups

What You Need

2 cups cooked
   garbanzos
1 onion
2 cloves garlic
1/2 t sweet basil
1/2 t parsley

3 ripe tomatoes or
   equivalent sauce
2-3 T olive oil
1 t salt
1/2 t tarragon
1 green pepper, chopped

What You Do

1. Saute sliced onion, pepper and minced garlic in olive oil.
2. Add herbs to taste.
3. Add tomatoes, simmer 2 minutes. Add drained garbanzos.
4. Pour into casserole, cover and bake at 325° for 1/2 hour.

CHINESE NOODLE TOFU CHEESE PIE
Yield: serves 2

What You Need

6 cups of water
1/2 cup POURABLE JACK
  CHEESE
1/2 lb. firm tofu
1 t basil

1 2-or-3 oz. pkg. Bean Thread
  (cellophane noodles)
1 T lemon juice
1/2 t salt
1/4 t garlic powder
1/2 t onion powder

What You Do

1. Boil bean thread in water for 5 minutes.
2. Drain bean thread well.
3. Mix POURABLE JACK CHEESE with the bean thread.
4. Press mixture evenly into a 9-inch pie plate, molding mixture along the sides as well.
5. Make RICOTTA STYLE TOFU FILLING (Book Publishing 1982) by mixing together remaining ingredients and mashing with a fork.
6. Fill the center of the bean thread pie shell with the Ricotta Tofu Filling.
7. Bake at 350° for 20 minutes or until heated through.

*Variation: Eliminate the Ricotta Style Filling and just bake a plain cheese pie. Replace bean thread with corn noodles or spaghetti.

144

BUCKWHEAT PIZZA and PESTO SAUCE
Adapted from *The Vegetarian Chef* by David Cohlmeyer
Yield: 1 pizza

What You Need

4 cups water
1 cup raw buckwheat
3/4 t salt
1/4 t salt
1/2 cup olive oil
1/2 cup filbert or pecan nuts
2 cups parsley
1 t fresh basil
3 cloves garlic
1 t lemon juice
1/2 cup water (use judgment to make a thick mixture)

What You Do

1. Combine 4 cups water, 1 cup raw buckwheat and 3/4 t salt.
2. Bring to boil, turn down and simmer 45 minutes.
3. Pour into a circular pizza pan or 11 x 13 cookie sheet and cool in refrigerator until solid.
4. To make topping, blend all other ingredients and spread over crust.
5. Decorate with TOFU STEAKS, cubed or TOFU COTTAGE CHEESE, red or green peppers, sliced onion circles, and/or black olives.
6. Bake at 350° for 15 minutes or until heated through.

BOSTON BAKED BEANS
Adapted from *Ten Talents*
Yield: 4-6 cups

What You Need

2 cups dry navy beans
3 T molasses
1 t salt
1/4 t garlic
2 T maple syrup
1 medium onion,
chopped and sauteed

What You Do

1. Cover navy beans with water, plus 2". Cook on low in crock pot, or simmer on stove for 2 hours or until tender
2. Then add other ingredients and cook for 1/2 hour more.

STIR FRY
Yield: serves 4

What You Need

1 lb. firm tofu
2 cups broccoli flowers
1 cup celery, slant out
1 garlic clove, minced
1 t onion powder

6 T yeast flakes
3 cups bok choy, chopped
1 large onion, sliced
1 t salt
1/2 t garlic powder

What You Do

1. Cut tofu into 1 inch cubes.
2. Toss cubes in breading meal of yeast flakes, onion powder, salt, and garlic powder.
3. Bake in oven on oiled cookie sheet at 350° until browned, about 15 minutes per side.
4. In frying pan or wok, saute in 2 T olive oil and 2 T water the following, in order: garlic, onion, celery, bok choy, and broccoli.
5. The combination of vegetables makes a mild but tasteful blend. Stir in tofu cubes.
6. Serve over brown rice, or serve alone or on alfalfa sprouts.
*Variation: Use cauliflower, red peppers, and other greens of your choice.

SPANISH RICE
Yield: serves 3 to 4

What You Need

1 medium onion, chopped
1 clove garlic, minced
1 t salt
1 cup brown rice, uncooked

1 small green pepper, diced
4 cups canned tomatoes with
juice

What You Do

1. Bring all ingredients to boil in covered sauce pan.
2. Reduce heat, and simmer one hour.
*Variation: After steps 1 & 2 may bake at 350° for 15 minutes.

MAIN DISHES AND GRAVIES

CEYLONESE RICE
Adapted from *The Strict Vegetarian Cookbook*
Yield: serves 4

What You Need

1 cup onion, chopped
1 cup water
3 cups cooked rice
1/2 t salt
1 t tarragon

1/2 cup carrot sticks, thin
10 oz. frozen peas
1 t parsley
1 t dill

What You Do

1. Steam onion and carrot sticks in 1/2 cup water.
2. Add remaining ingredients, heat through and serve.
*Variation: Top with 1 cup roasted cashews or almonds.

RATATOUILLE
Yield: 6 cups

What You Need

1 medium eggplant,
1 medium zucchini, sliced
4 tomatoes, chopped
2 T olive oil
1 t salt

1 medium onion, sliced
2 green peppers, sliced
1 garlic clove, minced
2 T water

What You Do

1. Peel and slice eggplant.
2. Bake eggplant on oiled cookie sheet for 15 minutes a side at 350°.
3. Saute onion and garlic in olive oil, or steam in fry pan with water.
4. Add zucchini and peppers, eggplant, tomatoes and salt.
5. Simmer covered for 1/2 hour to 45 minutes until liquid evaporates.
6. Can be eaten hot or cold.

MAIN DISHES AND GRAVIES

ENCHILADAS
Yield: 12 enchiladas

What You Need

12 corn tortillas
1 can mild chilies (optional)
2 recipes POURABLE JACK CHEESE

4 cups cooked lightly seasoned
   pinto or kidney beans

What You Do

1. Soften tortillas by wrapping in damp towel and warming in 250° oven for 10 minutes. Fill each tortilla with beans; roll, and lay with seam down on an oiled pan.
2. Mix chilies with POURABLE JACK CHEESE and pour over enchiladas-You may not need all of the cheese.
3. Bake at 350° for half an hour.
*Variation: Top with chopped raw onions and sliced olives.

EGGPLANT ROLLS
Yield: serves 2

What You Need

One 8-10" eggplant, peeled
1 cup yeast flakes
1/2 t salt
1 1/2 cups POURABLE JACK
   CHEESE
8 slices SLICEABLE JACK CHEESE

1/2 tsp garlic powder
1/2 tsp onion powder
1cup TOFU COTTAGE
   CHEESE

What You Do

1. Slice eggplant lengthwise from top to bottom into approximately 8 thin slices. Bread eggplant slices in breading meal, or mix together and use the seasonings in the recipe.
2. Oil 2 cookie sheets and bake eggplant at 350° for 20 minutes a side. Watch for burning, as slices will be thin. Let cool.
3. In each eggplant slice, place 2 T TOFU COTTAGE CHEESE and a strip of SLICEABLE JACK CHEESE or BAKED CHEESE SQUARES. Roll up and place in an 8 x 8 baking dish.
4. Pour over 1 1/2 cups JACK CHEESE. Bake at 350° for 30 min.

MAIN DISHES AND GRAVIES

BAKED POTATO

What You Need

1 T olive oil per potato   salt

What You Do

1. Bake potatoes. Split open. Add oil. Sprinkle with salt.

SCALLOPED POTATOES
Yield: serves 4

What You Need

6 potatoes   4 onions, cut in rings
salt to taste   3 cups CASHEW MILK
                              1 t paprika

What You Do

1. Boil potatoes for 20 minutes, then slice.
2. Steam onions for 10 minutes, cut in rings.
3. Layer in 9 x 9 dish the potatoes and onions, and sprinkle each
   potato layer with salt. Cover with milk. Sprinkle with paprika.
4. Bake at 350° for 1 hour.

BAKED STUFFED POTATOES
Yield: serves 6

What You Need

6 potatoes   1 cup broccoli flowers and
3 scallions   stems
1 cup parsley   1 t salt

What You Do

1. Bake potatoes for 1 hour at 400°. Saute remaining ingredients.
2. Cut potato in half. Remove potato and mix with broccoli.
3. Re-stuff potato skins and bake 15 more minutes.

MAIN DISHES AND GRAVIES

Burgers
ASPARGUS PATTIES
Adapted from *Ten Talents*
Yield: 6 patties

What You Need

1 1/2 cups asparagus, chopped raw or steamed
1/2 cup almonds blended to meal
1 cup grated carrots   1/2 cup thick nut or soy milk
1/2 small onion, chopped   1/2 t salt
1/2 t paprika   1 cup oats or
1/2 t thyme   1/2 cup potato starch

What You Do

1. Blend smooth milk, oats, onions and seasonings.
2. Mix all ingredients together. Drop by tablespoonfuls on an oiled baking sheet. Bake at 350° for 15 minutes on each side.

LENTIL BURGERS
Yield: 8 burgers

What You Need

1 1/2 cup dry lentils   4 cups of water
1 t salt   2 T olive oil, (optional)
1 onion, diced (optional)   1 t sage
1/2 t garlic powder   1 t onion powder

What You Do

1. Blend lentils to a fine meal. Saute onion in olive oil in a 2 quart pan. Add 4 cups of water, cover and bring to boil.
2. Add rest of herbs and turn burner to low.
3. Add dry lentil meal slowly, using a whip to keep from lumping.
4. Cook 1/2 hour on low, watching and stirring, as it will thicken and stick if you don't stir.
5. Pour into round plastic quart storage containers. Chill.
6. Pop out of container, slice into patties and bake on oiled cookie sheets 15 minutes per side at 350°.
7. Top with sliced onion, tomato and catsup, if you desire.

OAT BURGERS
Yield: 12 oat burgers

What You Need

3 cups water
1/4 cup soy sauce or
    Bragg's Liquid Aminos
3 cups rolled oats
1 medium onion, chopped

1/4 t garlic powder
1 t onion powder
1/2 cup sunflower seeds
1 t basil

What You Do

1. Simmer chopped onions in 2 T water until soft.
2. Add water, onion, soy sauce and seasonings.
3. Bring to boil.
4. Lower to medium heat and immediately pour in 3 cups of oats and stir.
5. Turn stove to simmer and cook 5 minutes.
6. Take from stove top and add 1/2 cup of sunflower seeds.
7. Let cool.
8. Shape into patties, using a quart canning jar ring as a shaper.
9. Bake on an oiled cookie sheet at 350° for 35 minutes then flip and continue to bake 15 minutes.
10. Serve with CATSUP and sliced raw onions.
11. Use wax paper to separate burgers for storage. You may freeze them.

*Variations:
1. Make meat balls for spaghetti sauce by adding 1-2 cups cooked millet or brown rice. Shape into balls and bake at 350° for 25 minutes, roll over and continue to bake 10-15 minutes
2. Omit basil and use 1/2 t thyme and 1/2 t sage.
3. Omit soy sauce and use 1/4 cup GAMASIO and 1/2 t salt.
Suggestion: You can purchase unfermented soy sauce in health food stores. Examples of brand names are Bragg's Liquid Aminos or Dr. Bonner and others. The standard brand of LaChoy is also unfermented.

TOFU SPROUT BURGER
Adapted from *Vegetarian Times*
Yield: 6 burgers

What You Need

2 cups firm tofu, mashed	1/4 cup sunflower seeds
2 cups alfalfa sprouts	1/4 grated carrots
1/2 onion, chopped	1/4 cup parsley, chopped
1/2 t salt	onion powder, garlic powder,
1/4 cup tahini	sage, or rosemary (optional)

What You Do

1. Blend sunflower seeds in a dry blender to meal.
2. Knead all ingredients well in a bowl until sprouts are evenly distributed.
3. Shape into patties with a canning jar ring.
4. Apply breading meal of your choice or bake plain.
5. Bake on oiled pan at 350° for 20 minutes per side or until brown, or bake on a griddle.
6. The burgers are fragile, so be careful as you turn them.
7. Burgers have a delicate taste much like a fish cake.

EGGPLANT TOFU BURGER
Adapted from *Vegetarian Times*
Yield: 8 burgers

What You Need

1/2 lb. firm tofu
1/4 t salt
1 cup minced onions
1/2 cup eggplant
1/2 cup nuts
1/2 to 1 cup corn flakes
   or cooked rice

1/4 cup tahini
1/4 cup fresh parsley, chopped
1 T Bragg's Liquid Aminos or 1
   soy sauce
1 t basil
1 t dill

What You Do

1. Peel and dice eggplant.
2. Boil in water to cover until tender. Drain well.
3. Mix with rest of ingredients. Form into patties.
4. Bake on oiled pan 20 minutes on each side at 350°.
*Variation: Eliminate eggplant for Nightshade-free TOFU SUN BURGER. Add 1/2 cup ground sunflower seeds. Or replace corn flakes or rice   with 2 T potato starch.

Gravies

CASHEW GRAVY
Reprinted from *The Country Life Natural Foods Cookbook*
Yield: 2 1/2 cups

What You Need

2 cups water
2 t onion powder
1/4 t garlic powder

1/2 cup cashews
1/2 t salt
1 T yeast flakes (optional)

What You Do

1. Blend smooth one cup of water with remaining ingredients.
2. Add remaining water.
3. Pour into saucepan and cook over medium heat, stirring constantly until thick.

EGGLESS EGG GRAVY
Yield: 1 and 3/4 cups

What You Need

1/4 cup cashews
2 T Bragg's Liquid Aminos
   or soy sauce
1 t onion powder
1/4 t salt

1/2 cup water
1/2 t garlic powder
1 T yeast flakes
1 cup SCRAMBLED TOFU

What You Do

1. Blend all ingredients except tofu in your blender.
2. Put in saucepan and bring to boil, stirring to keep the gravy smooth.
3. Add SCRAMBLED TOFU.
4. Heat through.
5. Serve over mashed potatoes or greens or toast.

TAHINI GRAVY
Yield: 1 cup

What You Need

2 T Bragg's Liquid Aminos or soy sauce
1 T potato starch   1 cup water
2 T tahini

What You Do

1. Blend all above and cook until thick (stir to keep from sticking).

GRAVY FOR MASHED POTATOES
Yield: 1 cup

What You Need

6 chopped scallions
1 clove minced garlic
1 T arrowroot

1 cup water or vegetable stock
Handful of parsley, chopped fine
1 T soy sauce

What You Do

1. Saute the chopped scallions and minced garlic in 1 T oil or 1/4 cup of water.
2. Add remaining ingredients and bring to boil, stirring with wire whip. Simmer for 10 minutes.

FLOURLESS GRAVY
Yield: 2 cups

What You Need

2 cups water
3 T potato starch
1/4 t garlic powder
1/4 t onion powder

1/2 t salt
2 t Bragg's Liquid Amino
    or soy sauce

What You Do

1. Bring ingredients to boil , stirring constantly with wire whip until thickened.
2. Adjust seasonings to your taste.

RICE OR MILLET GRAVY
Yield: 3 cups

1 cup cooked grain
2 cups water
1/2 t salt

1/4 cup nut or seed
2 t HOMESTYLE CHICKEN
    SEASONING

1. Blend all above ingredients until creamy in your blender.
2. Bring to boil, stirring with wire whip to keep smooth.
3. Adjust seasonings to taste, and serve.

Tofu Meat of the Field

TOFU STEAKS, SCRAMBLED TOFU, OILLESS TOFU MAYONNAISE, EGGLESS EGG SALAD, and TOFU CAROB PIE topped with TOFU WHIPPED CREAM. These are just a few of the possibilities that you can create with tofu. Tofu, a processed soybean product, has been available for 2,000 years - principally in China and Japan. For you "American made" fans, the American tofu industry is one of the few growing businesses within today's economic crisis. Tofu is a good source of protein, is low in calories, and is cholesterol- free. The real selling point is that tofu takes on the flavor of whatever you cook it with. If you add tofu to vegetables, it will pick up their flavors; or you can sweeten it and make a pudding, or add garlic, onion and lemon and make a salad dressing.

Tofu's variety is not only in taste but also in texture. Mash it and it looks like scrambled eggs. Slice and bake tofu and it becomes chewy. Blend tofu in your blender until creamy and it becomes a spread. Freeze it, defrost and drain, and the texture becomes like pasta or bread. There are even ice cream products made of tofu. Tofu is not just an oriental food which is limited to stir fry vegetables. It makes a great no-cholesterol cheese substitute for TOFU LASAGNA or CHEESECAKE. Any American barbecue will be a success with tofu burgers as the main entree, with everything on it. The typical rich Russian stroganoff lacks nothing when you replace the beef with tofu. So you have a taste and texture surprise each time you experiment with tofu.

Tofu is a dieter's delight, high in nutrition but low in calories. Compared to hamburger protein rich tofu has 1/4 as many calories, less fat, and more calcium. A nutritional taste treat awaits you.

For more information there are a number of cookbooks available. William Shurtleff's Book of Tofu, Cathy Bauer's Tofu Cookbook, and Louise Hagler's Tofu Cookery, are excellent recipe sources. Look in your supermarket's fresh produce department or deli for packaged tofu. Obtain fresh tofu from health food stores, if available. A new taste treat or a familiar friend, tofu will offer you a new dimension in cooking.

MAIN DISHES AND GRAVIES

TOFU YUNG AND GRAVY
Adapted from *Tofu Cookery* by Louise Haggler
Yield: serves 5-6

What You Need

1 1/2 cups snow peas or
    green beans
2 lbs. soft tofu, drained
1/4 cup soy sauce or
    1/4 cup Bragg's Liquid
    Aminos
1/3 cup potato starch

8 scallions, chopped or
    1 cup chopped onions
2 cups mung bean sprouts
1/4 cup water
8 oz. can water chestnuts,
    drained and sliced
3 T yeast flakes

What You Do

1. In a skillet steam the chopped snow peas, onions, and water chestnuts in 1/4 cup water for 5 minutes.
2. Add sprouts. Cover and steam 3 minutes. Take cover off and set aside.
3. Blend 1 1/2 lbs. tofu in soy sauce or Bragg's.
4. Pour blended tofu into a bowl and mix in 1/2 cup mashed tofu, 1/3 cup potato starch, and yeast flakes.
5. Add steamed vegetables and mix well.
6. Oil lightly two 11 x 15 cookie sheets.
7. Make patties of 1/2 cup each and place on cookie sheets.
8. Bake at 350° for 15 minutes each side, so that each side is lightly browned.
9. Serve over rice, noodles or mung bean thread topped with TOFU YUNG GRAVY (see next page).

MAIN DISHES AND GRAVIES

TOFU YUNG GRAVY
Adapted from *Tofu Cookery* by Louise Haggler
Yield: 2 cups

What You Need

2 cups water
2 T arrowroot or potato
   starch

1/4 cup Bragg's Liquid Aminos
   or soy sauce

What You Do

1. Mix all the above ingredients cold in a pan.
2. Use a wire whip to make mixture smooth.
3. Lightly boil 5 minutes, stirring continously.

ZUCCHINI PATTIES
©Book Publishing Co. 1982 (adapted)
Yield: serves 4-6

What You Need

1 large onion, sliced thin
1/4 cup fresh parsley
   chopped
3 cloves fresh garlic, minced
1 1/2 lbs. tofu
1 t Italian seasoning
1 t basil

4 medium zucchini, shredded
1 green pepper,
   chopped(optional)
1 t salt
1/4 cup potato starch or 6 T
   arrowroot
1/4 cup Bragg's Liquid Aminos

What You Do

1. Steam onion, zucchini, parsley and garlic 3-5 minutes.
2. Remove from heat.
3. Blend 1 lb. tofu with Bragg's or soy sauce.
4. In a separate bowl mix: 1/2 lb. mashed tofu, salt, potato starch.
   Stir in steamed vegetables.
5. Lightly oil two 11 x 15 cookie sheets.
6. Make patties of 1/2 cup each and place on sheets.
7. Bake at 350° for 15 minutes each side until lightly browned.
   Serve topped with your favorite tomato sauce.

MAIN DISHES AND GRAVIES

TOFU-RICE LOAF
Adapted from *The Country Life Natural Foods Cookbook*
Yield: 8 x 8 baking dish serves 6

What You Need

3 cups cooked brown rice
3 cups tofu, drained and
   mashed
1/2 t garlic powder
1T onion powder
1 t salt (optional)
1 t cumin
1/2 cup chopped walnuts
   (optional)

2 T water
2 T olive oil (optional)
2 cups chopped onions
1 T yeast flakes (optional)
2 T Bragg's Liquid Aminos
   or soy sauce
1/2 cup chopped fresh
   parsley or 2 T dried

What You Do

1. Saute onions in 2 T water and 2 T olive oil or 4 T water.
2. Place other ingredients in a bowl, add onions and mix well.
3. Bake in oiled casserole dish at 350° for 1 hour.
4. Serve plain or with a nut gravy.
*Variations: 1. Use 1 cup of cooked oatmeal and 1 1/2 cups of cooked rice instead of 3 cups rice.
2. Add mayonnaise to taste to leftovers and use as a sandwich spread or top with a lettuce leaf and decorate with a sprig of fresh parsley.

TOFU TACO SCRAMBLER

1. Warm 12 taco shells for 10 minutes at 300°.
2. Serve at the table with one recipe SCRAMBLED TOFU and various SALSA recipes.
3. Each person assembles their own taco, using Scrambled Tofu and Salsa.

TOFU STEAKS
Yield: steaks for two

What You Need

1 lb. firm or extra
  firm tofu
1 t onion powder

6 T yeast flakes
1/2 t garlic
1/2 t salt

What You Do

1. Cut tofu in half so that it is half its original thickness. Then slice 8 short strips per half.
2. Mix seasonings in a small plastic bag.
3. Add tofu strips and shake until tofu is well covered.
4. Brown lightly on oiled baking sheet at 350° 15-20 minutes per side.
5. Serve hot as a main dish. If you wish, put a tomato sauce or gravy over the steaks.

*Variation: 1. Cube tofu in 1 or 2" squares, toss in seasoning bag, bake and use in a stir-fry or pot pie.
2. Use the seasonings with thinnly sliced zucchini and bake as step 4.

YEAST-FREE TOFU STEAKS
Alternative to Yeast Breading Meal
Sesame Seed-Seaweed Breading Meal

What You Need

1/2 lb. tofu
2 T parsley flakes
1/4-1/2 t salt or kelp

2 T sesame seeds
1 T green nori flakes
1/2 t onion powder

What You Do

1. Blend sesame seeds in blender or nut grinder to make meal.
2. Follow steps 2 through 5 as noted in recipe for TOFU STEAKS above.

*Variation: Lightly toast Wakame seaweed in a dry frying pan and crumble into flakes and substitute for nori.

MAIN DISHES AND GRAVIES

SCRAMBLED TOFU
Yield: serves 2 generously

What You Need

1/2 t garlic powder
1 lb firm tofu,
  mashed
2-4 T yeast
  flakes

3/4-1 t onion powder
1/2 t salt
2 T chives (optional)
1/4 t tumeric for color

What You Do

1. Mix all ingredients and heat through.
2. Tasty hot or cold as a sandwich filling.
*Variation: 1. Dry roast 2 T sesame and sunflower seeds in frying pan and add to tofu.
2. NONIRRITATING CURRY SEASONING: 1 t coriander, 1 t cumin, 1/2 t salt, 1/2 t garlic powder, 1 t onion powder may be added.

TOFU VEGETABLE QUICHE
Reprinted from *Cooking with Natural Foods*

What You Need

1/2 cup chopped green pepper
1/2 cup pimentos
1/2 lb tofu
1 cup water
1 t salt
1 t sweet basil or Italian seasonings

1/2 cup sliced onions
1/2 cup diced carrots
1 cup cashews
1 t garlic
2 T arrowroot

What You Do

1.Saute vegetables (peppers, pimentos, onions, carrots) in small
  amount of water or oil.
2.Blend smooth remaining ingredients.
3.Mix together and pour into oiled pie plate.
4.Bake at 350° for 35 minutes.

MAIN DISHES AND GRAVIES

TEXTURED TOFU PROTEIN
Reprinted from *The Tofu Cookbook*
Yield: 1 cup

What You Need

1 lb firm tofu

What You Do

Place tofu in a plastic container without any water and freeze. When frozen the tofu will turn a yellowish color. Remove and defrost the tofu and squeeze out any water in a colander. One may use a microwave to speed up the thawing process. Put in a bowl and mash with a fork. Spread out on a cookie sheet in low oven (250°) until dehydrated. Use as you would textured vegetable protein. It will store unrefrigerated.

STROGANOFF
Adapted from *The Tofu Cookbook*
Yield: serves 4

What You Need

2 cups OIL-LESS TOFU MAYONNAISE
2 cups TEXTURED TOFU PROTEIN
1/2 cup water   1 onion, diced
2 T water   1 t salt
1 T dill weed   1 t onion powder
1/2 t garlic powder

What You Do

1. Saute 1 diced onion in 2 T water until onion softens.
2. Add 2 cups of textured tofu protein and lightly brown.
3. After a few minutes add all remaining ingredients excluding water.
4. Add the 1/2 cup of water to create a moist but not runny consistency.
5. Taste and adjust seasonings.
6. Serve over brown rice.

TOFU LASAGNA

Instead of using cheese on your lasagna noodles, mash 1 lb. of tofu with OIL-LESS TOFU MAYONNAISE to get texture of ricotta cheese. Substitute corn flat noodles or mung bean thread for wheat lasagna noodles and layer noodles, tomato sauce or pesto sauce, and tofu. When the corn flat noodles bake, the mixture sets like a noodle pudding.

TOFU POT PIE

Replace meat with tofu chunks, add more seasonings, and you have a low-fat, no cholesterol, high nutrition, low calorie entree.

SOUPS

SOUPS

Mung Bean Thread or Cellophane Noodles

The next time you pass by the oriental section in the grocery store, be on the lookout for packages of stiff white noodles that look like cellophane. Even though mung bean threads look refined, they are in fact a whole product. Mung bean flour is ground from the whole bean and used to make the bean threads. Bean threads are high in complex carbohydrates and are a good source of vitamin A and B vitamins, and a 1 oz. package contains 114 calories.

Soak the package of bean threads in enough water to cover it for five minutes. Drain well and cut up the threads with scissors into desired lengths. Cook in boiling water for 5 minutes, drain well and use in place of spaghetti. You can also add threads to soup to replace macaroni or grains, or use them instead of rice when serving a stir fry. Although bean threads may be cooked without soaking and cutting, they tend to stick together and are much harder to work with.

Native to India, mung beans spread to China, and have been cultivated in Asia since 1500 B.C. When the bean is sprouted, its food value increases by five times. According to research done by Sally Stone in The Brilliant Bean, when sprouted, mung beans even form vitamins C and B12, which are not found in the unsprouted bean. Sally Stone explains in her book that bean sprouts are easy to digest because the sprouting process turns the starches into simple sugars and the proteins into amino acids. In the sprouting process the green outer covering separates to reveal the white sprout. Mung bean sprouts, found in the fresh produce section of your grocery store, can replace tofu or meat in a stir fry, chow mein, or chop suey to give the needed protein. Bean sprouts steamed with onions and peppers is a simple and delicious meal served over rice or bean threads. Mung bean threads and sprouts are worth experimenting with and are easily available in most grocery stores, health food stores, or oriental specialty shops.

BEAN THREAD ORIENTAL SOUP
Reprinted from *Horn of the Moon Cookbook*
Yield: serves 4-6

What You Need

1 1/2 lbs. firm tofu
4 scallions or 1 onion, chopped
2 cups chopped bok choy
1 cup broccoli flowers
   and stems, chopped
3 cloves garlic, minced
1 cup carrots, sliced

7 cups of water or
   vegetable stock
1 pkg. (2.5 oz) mung bean
   threads
6 T Bragg's liquid Aminos or
   soy sauce

What You Do

1. Cut 1 1/2 lbs. of tofu into 2 inch cubes.
2. Bake cubes on oiled cookie sheet at 350° for 20 minutes each side.
3. Remove from oven; pour over the tofu 2 T Bragg's Liquid Aminos or soy sauce, and let marinate while cooking soup.
4. Cook the vegetables in the water until tender.
5. Add remaining ingredients.
6. Simmer 15 minutes, and serve.

BOUQUET GARNI
Yield: 1/2" by 3" muslin or cheesecloth bag

What You Need

2 dried bay leaves
1 clove garlic(optional)
1 sprig fresh thyme or 1 t dried

3 sprigs fresh parsley
   or 1 T dried

What You Do

1. Mix all ingredients together.
2. Place into a cheesecloth or muslin bag and tie closed.
3. Place bag in soups as a seasoning.
4. Remove before serving.

KALE VEGETABLE SOUP
Yield: serves 4-6

What You Need

4-6 potatoes, diced
8 cups kale, chopped
3 carrots, sliced
2 cloves fresh garlic, minced
1 cup cooked garbanzos or
  1 pkg. Tofu Pups
1/2 t basil
1/2 t dill
1 t salt

8 cups vegetable broth
  or water
1 large onion, diced
4 cups whole tomatoes
1/2 t ground fennel
1/2 t garlic powder
1/2 t ground celery seed
1 t tarragon

What You Do

1. In a 4 quart sauce pan simmer for 20 minutes: onions, fresh garlic, kale and carrots in broth.
2. Add potatoes. Bring to boil then simmer until potatoes become tender.
3. Add garbanzos, tomatoes and seasonings and simmer an additional 20 minutes to blend flavors thoroughly.

LENTIL SOUP
Yield: serves 4-6

What You Need

2 T olive oil
8 cups water
1 green pepper, diced
16 oz. can of tomatoes
1 t salt

2 T water
1 large Spanish onion, chopped
1 lb. or 2 2/3 cups dry lentils
1 pimento, drained and diced
4 medium carrots, diced

What You Do

1. Saute in olive oil and 2 T water: onion, green pepper, pimento.
2. Mix all ingredients in soup pot.
3. Bring to boil; reduce heat and simmer on low for two hours. Thick and delicious!

SOUPS

SPLIT PEA SOUP
Yield: 4 to 5 cups

What You Need

1 lb. or 2 2/3 cups split peas
8 cups water
1 t salt
1/2 t garlic powder

1 bay leaf
2 t onion powder
1/2 t ground rosemary

What You Do

1. Cook peas, water and bay leaf overnight in crock pot. Set on low, or simmer on stove 1-2 hours.
2. Now add seasonings to soup and cook 1/2 hour more.
*Variation:
1. Rinse 1/4 cup Hijiki Arame briefly with fresh water.
2. Soak 1/2 hour.
3. Drain hijiki. May rinse a second time to reduce the sodium content.
4. Add to soup and simmer 15 minutes.
5. Hijiki, which has a mild nutlike flavor and crisp texture, will expand when soaked.

BARLEY AND SPLIT PEA SOUP
Yield: serves 4-6

What You Need

8 cups water
1 medium onion or leek
2 ribs celery
3 sprigs parsley
1/2 t salt

2 large carrots
1/2 cup barley
1/2 cup dried split peas
2 cups chopped kale or cabbage
bay leaf

What You Do

1. Put in covered pot, bring to boil, turn down and simmer 1 hour: water, barley, split peas, bay leaf and salt.
2. Dice vegetables and add to soup; simmer 1/2 hour.

ALLAH'S UKRAINIAN BORSCHT
Yield: serves 4-6

What You Need

1/2 cup dry kidney beans
4 cups water
1 stalk celery, diced
1 onion, chopped
1 T dill
1 minced clove garlic

1 cup cabbage, chopped
3 medium potatoes in chunks
2 cups red beets in chunks
1 cup green pepper, chopped
1 16 oz can tomatoes

What You Do

1. Soak kidney beans in 3 cups water 6-8 hours. Drain.
2. Bring to a boil water, kidney beans, celery, onion.
3. Simmer for 1 1/2 hours.
4. Add cabbage, potatoes, red beets, and green pepper.
5. Simmer until vegetables are cooked.
6. Add tomatoes. When soup bubbles, remove from heat.
7. Add dill and garlic. Serve.

CREAM OF CARROT SOUP
Yield: serves 1

What You Need

1/2 t salt
3 T yeast flakes
2 T peanut butter or other
   nut butter

2 cups soy milk or
   CASHEW MILK
2 medium carrots, chopped
1/2 t onion powder

What You Do

1. Blend all above ingredients in your blender.
2. Bring to boil, turn down and simmer 10 minutes. Serve.

CREAM OF ASPARAGUS SOUP
Yield: serves 4

What You Need

2 cups water
4 small chopped parsnips
1 T dill

1-2 cups chopped asparagus
1/2 cup cashew pieces
salt to taste

What You Do

1. Steam asparagus and parsnips in 1 cup water until tender.
2. Blend 1/2 cup of cashews and 1 cup of water until creamy.
3. Add steamed vegetables 1 cup broth and blend.
4. Reheat in a saucepan, adding dill and salt to taste.
5. Serve hot or cold.

LIMA BEAN CHOWDER
Adapted from *The Country Life Natural Foods Cookbook*
Yield: serves 4-6

What You Need

1 diced onion
3 cups diced potatoes
1/2 cup whole kernel corn
1 t dill
1/4 t garlic powder

2 cups limas, frozen or fresh
1 1/2 t onion powder
1 T potato starch
4 cups soy milk
1/2 t salt or to taste

What You Do

1. Cook until tender in small amount of water, onion, potatoes, corn and limas.
2. Blend remaining ingredients.
3. Add to first mixture and heat through.

SOUPS

CORN-POTATO CHOWDER
Yield: serves 4

What You Need

6 cups water
1-2 onions, sliced
2 cups celery, chopped
1 cup fresh parsley,
   chopped fine
1 t garlic powder
1 t salt or to taste

4-6 cups potatoes, diced
2-4 cups corn
2 t basil
1 t dill weed
2 T chives
3 T yeast flakes (optional)
1 cup cashew pieces

What You Do

1. In a saucepan place all ingredients except cashews and 1 cup of water.
2. Bring to boil and then simmer until potatoes become tender.
3. Blend water and cashews until creamy. Add to soup as a cream to thicken.

LEEK AND POTATO SOUP
Yield: serves 4

What You Need

3 cups leeks, sliced
1 large onion, diced
6-8 cups broth or water
1 cup water
2 t dill weed
salt to taste

3 large garlic cloves, minced
7 potatoes, cut in chunks
1 cup cashew pieces
6 T chives, minced
1 T basil

What You Do

1. Steam garlic and onions in 1/2 cup of water.
2. Add broth and leeks and potatoes.
3. Bring to boil and simmer until potatoes become tender.
4. Blend 1 cup cashews and 1 cup of water until creamy.
5. Add cashew cream to soup and add seasonings.
6. Simmer 10 minutes to blend flavors.

171

GAZPACHO SOUP
Yield: 5 cups

What You Need

1 cup chopped tomatoes
1/2 cup chopped celery
1/4 cup chopped scallions
1 T chives
1 T lemon juice
1/2-1 t salt to taste

2 cups tomato or V-8 juice
1/2 cup chopped green pepper
1/2 cup chopped cucumber
2 T snipped fresh parsley
2 T olive oil

What You Do

1. Combine in a glass bowl, cover and chill.

FRUIT SOUP
Yield: 3 quarts

What You Need

2 bananas
1 cup dried apricots
3 T tapioca

4 cups unsweetened
   pineapple juice
1 pint strawberries

1 20-ounce can unsweetened pineapple chunks
1 20-ounce can unsweetened peaches, chopped

What You Do

1. Simmer on low to soften 1 cup dried apricots in 1 cup juice.
2. Cool and blend in blender, adding 2 cups more juice or water to make a thick apricot nectar.
3. In a 4-quart pot mix 1 cup pineapple juice and 3 T tapioca. Mix and simmer until tapioca thickens and clears 3-5 minutes.
4. Turn off heat and add remaining pineapple juice. Let cool.
5. Add pineapple, peaches and apricot nectar. Chill.
6. Before serving, slice 2 bananas and mix into soup.
7. Add sliced strawberries to float on the top.

Side Dishes and Cheeses

Instead of Spinach

Spinach's popularity as the top dark leafy green has overshadowed other candidates, such as collards, kale, mustard, and turnip greens, which also excel in nutritional value. Oxalic acid is found in dark leafy green vegetables as is calcium, iron and vitamins A and C. During digestion oxalic acid combines with calcium and forms calcium oxalate, an insoluble compound. The oxalic acid binds up the calcium, which causes the calcium to pass out of the body unabsorbed.

Spinach, beet greens and Swiss chard have 8 times as much oxalic acid as they do calcium. Most of the calcium will be carried out of the body without being absorbed because of the calcium oxalate that is formed. In collards, kale, turnip and mustard greens, and broccoli, calcium out numbers oxalic acid 42 to 1. Consequently, collards, kale, mustard and turnip greens win out over spinach in calcium absorption.

Variety is a principle that needs to be highlighted in your choice of greens. One cup of collards has as much calcium as one cup of milk, as much iron as 1/4 cup of raisins, as much vitamin C as 1 1/3 oranges and as much vitamin A as two carrots. At only 55 calories per cup, collards deserve the greens top ribbon award.

Because the allergic person may be vitamin deficient during elimination diets, or as a result of avoiding foods that cause sensitivity, it is especially important to choose foods that are storehouses of nutrition. Dark leafy greens fill this requirement. Experiment with different greens with your family. Chop the fresh greens up in soup or add them to your stir fry. Begin with just a little and mix the greens in with other more acceptable vegetables, like mashed potatoes or carrots. Use your favorite cream sauce or salad dressing or lemon juice over the greens.

Have your children grow greens in the garden. Bok choy especially grows well. As they cultivate and weed and observe the sturdy plants, and pick the harvest, they may be more willing to eat these powerhouses of nutrition.

SAUTEED GREENS

What You Need

1 onion-chopped
2 T olive oil
2 garlic cloves
1/4 cup water

1-2 lbs. collards, kale, or bok
choy
1/2 t salt

What You Do

1. Saute onions and minced garlic in olive oil until onions are soft.
2. Wash greens and chop to bite size pieces.
3. Add water to onions and place chopped greens on top of onions.
4. Cover and lower heat to steam 15 to 20 minutes.
5. Season to taste with salt.

KALE SOUFFLE
Yield: serves 4

What You Need

1 1/2 lbs. kale
1/2 lb. tofu
1/2 t onion powder
2 t dill

1 onion, chopped
1/2 t salt
1/2 t garlic powder
1 cup water

What You Do

1. Steam kale and onion in 1/2 cup water.
2. Drain. Save water for other recipes as a broth.
3. With a knife and fork, cut kale into small pieces.
4. Blend the remaining ingredients.
5. Mix kale and tofu in pie plate.
6. Bake 350° for 30 minutes.
*Variation: Replace kale with 10 oz. package frozen spinach.

WINTER SQUASH AND GREEN SURPRISE
Yield: 5 cups

What You Need

1/4 cup chopped onion
1 lb. cooked greens,
  chopped (spinach, kale, etc.)
1 t salt

3 cups cooked winter squash
yeast flakes to taste
1 T olive oil
1 t basil

What You Do

1. Saute onions in olive oil or water.
2. Add remaining ingredients and cook 15 minutes.
3. The surprise is how good it tastes!

MICROWAVE PARSNIPS AND DILL
Yield: serves 3 to 4

What You Need

6-8 medium parsnips
1 T dill weed

1/4 cup water
salt to taste

What You Do

1. Peel and slice parsnips.
2. Layer in 1 quart glass casserole with 1/4 cup water.
3. Sprinkle with salt and dill weed.
4. Cook in microwave for 5 minutes at medium.
5. Check and stir, then cook 5 minutes longer.
6. Repeat again if parsnips are not tender.

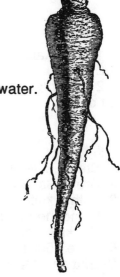

MARY'S VEGETABLE SAUCE
Yield: serves 4

What You Need

6 medium carrots
1 1/2 medium parsnips
3 sticks celery
1/2 t salt
2-3 onion, chopped
4 red peppers, chopped

1/2 t ground fennel
1 t basil
1 T Italian seasoning
3/4 cup water
3 cloves garlic, minced
2 T Bragg's Liquid Aminos
   or soy sauce

What You Do

1. In a pressure cooker, place carrots, fennel, parsnips, basil, celery, Italian seasoning, salt and 1/2 cup water.
2. Pressure cook for 45 minutes.
3. Saute 2 or 3 chopped onions and 3 cloves minced garlic in 1/4 cup water.
4. Add 4 chopped red peppers. Simmer until soft.
5. Put everything through food processor or blender, add the Braggs.
6. Use as a non-tomato alternative for Lasagna.
7. For a nightshade replacement sauce, use 2 beets in place of red peppers. Cook beets along with other veggies in pressure cooker.

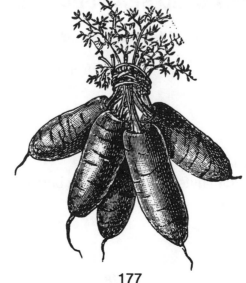

SIDE DISHES AND CHEESES

SUSHI
Yield: 4 sushi

What You Need

1 lb. tofu
1/2 t salt
1/2 t onion powder
4 nori sheets

1/2 t onion powder
1/2 t garlic powder
1 avocado, mashed

What You Do

1. Toast 4 nori sheets individually over open gas flame or electric burner. Do not touch the nori directly to the burner. As nori toasts, it will turn green.
2. Make TOFU COTTAGE CHEESE. Mash: tofu, onion powder, salt, and garlic powder.
3. Mash one avocado.
4. Lay nori sheet down and spread with 2 T avocado.
5. Top the avocado with 1/4 cup cottage cheese, spread evenly.
6. Top with alfalfa sprouts.
7. Roll up and with a sharp knife cut nori roll in half and then cut each half into three pieces.
8. Turn each piece up on end so that you can see the swirl.
9. Arrange on a plate.

TOASTED SEAWEED CHIPS

What You Need

wakame
nori fronds

kelp fronds

What You Do

1. Preheat oven to 250°.
2. Lay seaweeds out on a cookie sheet.
3. Toast 10 to 20 minutes to crisp but not burned. Watch carefully.

Facts On Casein And Soy Cheese

The ingredient list of processed foods offers a challenge for a nutrition detective. After investigating into casein, calcium or sodium caseinate and rennet, I am better able to make a choice in purchasing a product with these ingredients.

According to the encyclopedia, casein does not occur in a free state in milk, but is combined with calcium in a compound known as calcium caseinate. Casein, a white amorphous phosphoprotein, can be freed from its union with calcium by treating the milk with acids or adding rennet, a culture which contains an enzyme which curdles milk. The casein becomes an isolated protein and therefore does not contain the lactose or cholesterol of its original source, dry skim milk.

Sodium caseinate, the sodium salt of casein, is considered by the dairy industry and regulatory agencies as a chemical or food additive rather than a dairy product. Using this criteria it is permitted as a major ingredient on foods labeled "nondairy". According to the *Jewish Dietary Laws of Kashruth,* which regulates the kosher stamp of approval on "pareve" foods, any product containing casein is considered a dairy product, because casein is a skim milk derivative. Interestingly, fish and eggs are not considered meat products and can be used in "pareve" foods.

Casein's binding quality adds to the smooth texture of cheese, as well as the taste and the mouth feel. Casein gives cheese its melting and shredding quality. Casein makes up approximately 25% of hard cheeses and 20% of soy cheeses. Imported from New Zealand and Australia, casein is used for industrial purposes such as adhesive glues, binders in cold water paint, and to form plastics for buttons.

Rennet is the lining membrane of the fourth stomach of unweaned mammals - calves, lambs, goats, and pigs. Rennet is now commercially prepared in a microorganism form. VMC Corporation in Weehawken, New Jersey, produces a pure culture of liquid rennet derived from mushrooms. Rennet is used in hard cheese, as well as soft cheeses such as cottage cheese and mozzarella, but not ricotta. You would need to contact each company individually to know if they are using synthetic, vegetable or animal rennet.

Nondairy cheeses are expensive. The best prices are found in buying the cheeses in bulk through cooperatives. Because the cheeses are perishable they are not sold through mail order but through retail stores.

SIDE DISHES AND CHEESES

American Natural Snacks, producers of Soya Kass, claims that theirs is a no-rennet soy cheese, but they do list calcium caseinate on their ingredient list. The calcium caseinate has had the lactose removed by a mechanical rather than a chemical process.

Protein can be extracted from the soybean to form a soy protein isolate that can bind the product together. Soyco Foods, a division of Galaxy Cheese Co., is marketing Soymage as totally free of casein. The first ingredient is tofu and the second ingredient is soy protein isolate. It does shred, and there is a subdued melting action, but the bubbling action of dairy cheese is missing.

Piz Soy, a frozen pizza, has a mozzarella-type topping made from another Soyco product. Fifty-one percent of the mozzarella topping is tofu, and casein is the third ingredient after soy oil.

No Moochee is a nondairy cheese made from sesame tahini, pimento, water, coconut oil, olive oil, nutritional yeast, lemon juice, salt and herbs. It comes frozen, and *Whole Life Magazine* (June/July 1987) gave No Moochee an excellent review. No Moochee is not as readily available as the soy cheeses, but you can contract the distributor that is listed in the appendix.

Reference:
1. Bellizio, Jim, H.T.L. Inc, Correspondence, February 1988.
2. Goetz, Philip, editor, *Encyclopedia Britannica,* Vol. 2, p. 512,1986.
3. Medoff, Marc, "It's True, Casein-Free Nondairy Cheese is a Reality," *Whole Life,* June/July 1987.
4. Parker, Gus, *Garelick Farms*, phone conversation February 1988.
5. Savar, Robert, *The Original Pizsoy*, correspondence, Jan 21,1988.
6. Van Rysdam, Casex, American Natural Snacks, correspondence. Feb 1,1988.
7. Wade Cheryl, Soyco Foods, correspondence, Jan 8,1988.

SIDE DISHES AND CHEESES

SUNFLOWER PIMENTO CHEESE
Adapted from *The Country Life Natural Foods Cookbook*
Yield: 2 cups

What You Need

1 cup water
1/2 cup pimentos
3 T yeast flakes
2 T sesame seeds
1 t onion powder
1 1/4 t salt

3/4 cup sunflower seeds or
 cashews
1/4 cup lemon juice
1/4 t dill seed
1/8 t garlic powder

What You Do

1. Blend all ingredients until smooth.
2. Use as sauce over macaroni or steamed broccoli or cauliflower.

*Variation: To make brick cheese eliminate the 1 cup of water in the recipe above and mix 2 T agar flakes or 2 t agar powder in 1 1/2 cups of water. Bring to boil and then let cool. Blend all ingredients until creamy. Pour into a mold and chill until firm.

POURABLE JACK CHEESE
Yield: 2 1/2 cups

What You Need

1 cup water
1 t salt
3 T yeast flakes
1/4 cup lemon juice

1 cup cashews
1/8 t garlic powder
1 t onion powder
3 T finely grated carrot

What You Do

1. Blend all ingredients until thick and creamy.
2. Use as a sauce over macaroni, broccoli, cauliflower or enchiladas.

SLICEABLE JACK CHEESE
Reprinted from *The Joy of Cooking Naturally*
Yield:1 quart

What You Need

1 cup water
2 cups cashews
1/2 cup yeast flakes
2 t onion powder
3 T finely grated carrot
1/2 t garlic powder

1 1/2 cup boiling water
1/3 cup plus 1 rounded T Emes
   unflavored gelatin
1/2 cup lemon juice
1 or 1 1/2 t salt

What You Do

1. Soak gelatin and 1 cup water in blender.
2. Pour boiling water over soaked gelatin and cool briefly, then blend to dissolve.
3. Add cashews and blend until creamy.
4. Add remaining ingredients and blend again until creamy.
5. Pour into a quart mold.
6. Cover and refrigerate 6-8 hours until firm.
7. Slice and use as sandwich filling or on crackers.
*Variation: Substitute 1 pimento for grated carrot for a darker color.
*Serving Suggestions:
a. Potato-au-gratin - Use baked or boiled potatoes; open potato and spread sliced cheese on top. Broil for 2 minutes or toast in toaster oven or in microwave 2 minutes at medium. Cheese will melt.
b. Melt on steamed cauliflower or broccoli.

MILLET CHEESE
Yield: 4 cups

What You Need

1 t dill seed
1/2 cup cashews
1/4 cup sesame seeds
1/2 cup yeast flakes
1 t onion powder
1/2 t garlic powder

1 cup hot cooked millet
1cup water
1/2-1 t salt
1/2 cup lemon juice
1/4 cup canned pimentos

What You Do

1. Blend all ingredients smooth. Use more water if needed.
2. Refrigerate to set.
3. Good spread on crackers, or used for pizza topping.

BAKED CHEESE SQUARES
Yield: 24 squares

What You Need

1/2 cup tahini
1/2 t salt
1/2 cup fresh carrot or
1/4 cup canned pimento

1/2 cup yeast flakes
1/4 cup potato starch
1 cup water

What You Do

1. Blend all ingredients until creamy.
2. Pour on oiled cookie sheet. Bake 20 minutes at 350°.
3. Remove from oven and score into squares.
*Variation: Use 2 T potato starch instead of 1/4 cup, increase water by 1/2 cup, and pour into frying pan. Bring to boil, stirring constantly with wire whip. Turn down immediately and simmer 5 minutes. Delicious as a cheese gravy over cauliflower or broccoli, or on bread as grilled cheese alternative.

SALADS AND DRESSINGS

Salads and Dressings

Salads And Simplicity

Simplicity is an important goal for people with food sensitivities. Raw green and red sweet pepper sticks, alfalfa sprouts, parsley, cabbage, grated beets or carrots, and avocado are examples of nutritional excellence. Lettuce, cucumber, radish, and celery are crunchy, fibrous and low in calories, but not high in nutritional value. Pick your raw vegetables and fruits with a focus on their nutritional makeup. How much vitamin C, A, or iron, calcium, etc., do they have? It would be a worthwhile investment to purchase a book listing the nutritive values of foods. The United States Department of Agriculture publishes such a listing. When you are on a restricted diet, it is important that your food choices be of a high nutritional quality.

An example of a simple salad would be grated beets, grated carrots, and alfalfa sprouts arranged into 1/3 sections in a bowl and topped with fresh parsley sprigs. The moistness of the grated vegetables can be a substitute for a dressing. I usually try to serve a raw vegetable that I have used in my menu as a cooked vegetable. There is simplicity in food type but variety in texture.

GARBANZO SALAD
Yield: 1 1/2 cups

What You Need

1/2 cup chopped onion
  and celery
1/2 t onion powder
OIL-LESS TOFU
  MAYONNAISE

1 cup cooked drained garbanzos
1/2 t salt
1/4 t garlic powder
dry roasted sunflower seeds

What You Do

1. Mix ingredients, adding tofu mayonnaise to desired consistency.
2. Sprinkle with dry roasted sunflower seeds.

HUMMUS
Yield: 2 cups

What You Need

1/3 cup lemon juice
3 cloves garlic
1 t salt
1 t onion powder (optional)

1/4 cup bean juice or water
1 1/2 cups cooked garbanzos
1/3 cup tahini

What You Do

1. Blend all ingredients in a blender.
2. Chill.
3. Use as a dip for fresh vegetables, salad dressing, or sandwich spread.

POTATO SALAD
Yield: serves four

What You Need

6 - 8 potatoes
2 stalks celery, chopped
salt to taste
parsley

1 medium onion, chopped
1 cup OIL-LESS TOFU
    MAYONNAISE

What You Do

1. Steam or boil potatoes.
2. Drain potatoes when tender.
3. Cool and peel and cut into small cubes.
4. Add chopped celery, chopped onion and tofu mayonnaise.
5. Salt to taste and add parsley for decoration.

TOFU COTTAGE CHEESE
Yield: 1 cup

What You Need

2 cup tofu
1 T chives, chopped
pinch garlic powder

1 t onion powder
1/2 t salt
1/2-1 cup OIL-LESS TOFU
MAYONNAISE

What You Do

1. Mash tofu, garlic powder, onion powder, and salt with fork.
2. Add mayonnaise to desired texture. Add chives. Chill.
*Variation: TOFU EGGLESS EGG SALAD. Add 1/2 t celery seed,
1/8 t paprika, 1 minced green pepper, 1 rib celery chopped finely,
2 - 3 scallions or one small onion minced, and add parsley,
chives or grated carrot for variety.
*Variation: TOFU STUFFED TOMATO STARS. Cut the top off a
tomato and make a pointed design of top edges. Take out seeds
and pulp and stuff with tofu cottage cheese and garnish with
fresh parsley and olives.

SALSA
Adapted from *The Salsa Book* by Jacqueline McMahon
Yield: serves 4

What You Need

1 stalk celery
1 t lemon juice
2 cloves garlic, minced
1 t oregano
5 - 6 scallions or 1 small
  onion
1/4 t salt

4 cups plum tomatoes, drained
1 green pepper, chopped
  coarsely
1/2 t cumin
2 T canned mild chilies
  (optional)
4 - 5 T cilantro or parsley

What You Do

1. Chop and simmer for 10 - 20 minutes.
2. Serve as dip for corn chips, as a side dish, or as a dressing.

RAW CONFETTI SALSA SALAD
Adapted from *The Salsa Book* by Jacqueline McMahon
Yield: serves 4

What You Need

1 t oregano
1/4 t salt
3 - 4 T chopped parsley
2-3 cloves garlic, minced
5 carrots, shredded
1/4 cup lemon juice
2 T olive oil

1 small zucchini, shredded
1 red bell pepper, chopped
1 bunch scallions, minced, using
  part of green tops
1 - 2 chopped mild chilies
  (optional)

What You Do

1. Chop vegetables and mix in glass bowl with oregano, and salt.
2. Add oil, lemon juice and chilies. Chill.

RAW SALSA SALAD
Adapted from *The Salsa Book* by Jacqueline McMahon
Yield: serves 4

What You Need

5 medium tomatoes
1/3 cup onions
2 T olive oil
2 T lemon juice
3 T fresh chopped or
  snipped cilantro or
  parsley

2 cloves garlic
1 red or green pepper
Juice of 1 lime (optional)
1 T canned mild green chilies
  (optional)
1 t oregano
salt to taste

What You Do

1. Peel 5 medium tomatoes.
2. Chop vegetables. Mix all ingredients.
3. Let marinate at least two hours before serving. Tastes better
   the longer it marinates - up to 4 days. Refrigerate.

QUINOA TABOULI SALAD
Adapted from *Quinoa the Supergrain*
Yield: serves 4

What You Need

1 cup dry quinoa
3 cups water
1/2 cup fresh parsley
2 cloves garlic
1/2 t basil
1/4 cup lemon juice

4 cups tomatoes (optional)
1/2 cup scallions
1 T fresh mint or 1/2 t dried mint
1/2 t salt
1/4 cup olive oil

What You Do

1. Rinse thoroughly quinoa, and drain.
2. Lightly boil covered quinoa and water for 30 minutes.
3. Chop the tomatoes, scallions, parsley, mint, and garlic.
4. Put chopped vegetables and 2 cups cooked quinoa into a glass bowl.
5. Mix in basil, salt, olive oil, and lemon juice.
6. Pour over vegetables and marinate at least 2 hours.

PINEAPPLE-CARROT GEL
Yield: serves 4 - 6

What You Need

3 T Emes gelatin
1/2 cup walnut halves

4 cups pineapple juice
2 cups finely grated carrot

What You Do

1. Soak gelatin and pineapple juice 2 minutes in saucepan.
2. Bring to boil and turn off burner.
3. Add grated carrot.
4. Line the bottom of your mold with walnut halves.
5. Pour in gelatin juice mixture.
6. Chill in your refrigerator to solidify.
7. You can substitute Emes gelatin with 2 T agar powder or 4 T agar flakes.

SALADS AND DRESSINGS

BACON-LIKE LETTUCE AND TOMATO
Yield: 1 serving

What You Need

1 large tomato
1 T OIL-LESS TOFU MAYO
1 large lettuce leaf or handful of alfalfa sprouts

2 dried pieces seaweed-
wakame, nori, or kelp

What You Do

1. Toast seaweed on dry cookie sheets at 250° for 10 minutes. Watch carefully.
2. Place large lettuce leaf or sprouts on a plate.
3. Top with toasted seaweed then tomato and mayonnaise.
4. Eat as a salad or topping for waffle or crackers.

All Fats Are Not Created Equal
What are the best fats to eat? Every whole, natural plant food has a percentage of fat - some more, some less. Plant foods that have high percentages of fats are nuts, seeds, avocados, olives, and coconuts. Refined free fats, such as vegetable oils and margarines, are made from whole foods. The processing procedures extract the concentrated free fat, leaving the fiber and bulk to be used for animal feed or industrial manufacturing. Olive oil is the preferred oil, because it is the closest to a whole food in comparison with other oils. Plant oils are preferred over animal fats because of the percentage of filth and disease in animals. Cotton seed oil is objectionable because the cotton plants are heavily sprayed with insecticides. All fats are not created equal. Fats as they occur naturally in the whole plant are superior to refined fats.

The typical American eats 40% of his daily calories in fat and 25% in refined sugars. That adds up to 100 lbs of fat per person per year and 130 lbs of sugar per person per year. That 40% of the total daily fat calories only involves 8 tablespoons, but adds up to 1,000 calories. The American Cancer Society recommends that Americans lower their total fat intake from the current 40% figure to 25%. The late Nathan Pritikin, famous for his successful Longevity Centers, allowed no free fats, including nuts, olives or avocados, for his heart and cancer patients. His patients still absorbed 7 - 8% fat from their whole food diets. If you use 10%

free fats in your daily diet, you will be using 2 tablespoons of fat, which adds up to 250 calories. A little fat goes a long way. Whether you choose to follow the more liberal American Cancer Society guidelines or the more restrictive requirements of the Pritikin Program, the key is lowering and limiting your fat intake.

It is interesting to note that Eskimos living in Alaska subsisted on a high animal fat diet and yet had little or no degenerative diseases, until the Al-Can Highway connected isolated areas of Alaska with the more populated areas. Now that sugar, processed foods and refined oils have been made available, the Eskimos are suffering from degenerative diseases such as gallstones, diabetes, acne, heart disease, and tooth decay. It is important to be aware of the causal effects of eating excessive amounts and combinations of free fats, refined sugars, and white flour to the introduction of disease.

What does this mean for the allergic person? Fats, in any form, are a concentrated food and overuse clogs the blood stream. If your body gets overloaded with fats and/or sugar, your defense system is weakened. We need to give our immune system all the advantages we can give it. Putting fats into proper perspective is important. The bulk of your daily calories should come from eating foods high in carbohydrates, such as whole grains, vegetables and fruits. This should account for 60 - 80% of your total daily calories. Glean 15% of your protein requirement from combining grains, beans and nuts. Fats come in last place, supplying only 10% of your needed daily calories. Many foods that give Americans allergy problems are processed foods that combine fats and sugars, and refined flour. Cake, cookies, doughnuts, pastries, ice cream, milk shakes, candy, cheese cakes, and others are all to be avoided. Something better is available in the recipes that follow. Contented and healthful living is not an accident; rather it is an achievement, an accomplishment. Yes, it takes time to research, time to search out new foods, time to cook. But the time invested is well spent as your dividends of improved health are seen.

References:
1. Coulter, James, *Eating for the 80's: A Complete Guide to Vegetarian Nutrition*, Hartbarger and Neil, 1982.
2. Davis, Thomas, *Your Life and Health*, "The National Research Council Says: Reduce Cancer Risk Through Diet", Oct. 1982.
3. *Time Magazine*, "Fat of the Land", Feb. 13,1961, pp. 48-52.
4. *Woman's Day*, "Cancer Prevention", Feb. 8,1983.
5. Wright, Irving, Dr., "Prevention of Atherosclerotic Diseases", *Report of the InterSociety Commission for Heart Diseases*, Vol. 42,1972, p. 34.

OIL-LESS TOFU MAYONNAISE
Yield: 1 cup

What You Need

1 cup soft or silken
  tofu, drained
2 T lemon juice
1/2 t salt

1/4 cup water
1/2 t garlic powder
1 t onion powder

What You Do

1. Combine all ingredients and blend until smooth.
*Variation: For richer taste, add 2 T olive oil. For DILL PARSLEY MAYONNAISE, add 1/4 cup fresh parsley and 1/2 cup fresh dill weed. For RUSSIAN DRESSING, add 1/4 cup CATSUP.

POPPY SEED DRESSING
Reprinted from *Newstart Homestyle*
Yield: 3/4 to 1 cup

What You Need

3 T orange juice
2 T honey or 4 - 5 dates
1 T poppy seeds
1/2 t celery salt
grated onion to taste

2 T lemon juice
1/2 cup cashew nuts
1/2 t paprika
salt to taste
1/4 - 1/2 cup water

What You Do

1. Blend smooth all ingredients but the poppy seeds.
2. Pour into a container and stir in poppy seeds.

TAHINI DRESSING
Yield: 2 cups

1 cup tahini
1 T lemon juice
1/2 t salt

1 1/4 cup water
1/4 t garlic powder

1. Blend well.

192

ZERO SALAD DRESSING
Reprinted from *Newstart Homestyle*
Yield: 1/2 cup

What You Need

1 t toasted sesame seeds
1 t parsley
1 t dehydrated or flaked onion
1/4 t salt

1 fresh tomato or 1/2 cup
   tomato juice
1/2 t sweet basil

1. Roast the sesame seeds in a dry pan on medium to low heat until they pop. Blend all ingredients in your blender.

HERB DRESSING
Adapted from *The Horn of the Moon Cafe Cookbook*
Yield: 2 cups

What You Need

1/2 cup parsley, chopped
2 t dill weed
1 t chives
1/4 t celery seed

1/3 cup lemon juice
1 cup oil
1/4 t salt
2 large garlic cloves

1. Blend well in blender.

SUNNY SOUR CREAM
Yield: 1 1/2 cups

What You Need

3/4 cup sunflower seeds
2 - 3 T lemon juice
1/4 t garlic powder

3/4 cup water
1/2 t salt
1/2 t onion powder

What You Do

1. Blend all the ingredients in a blender.
2. Adjust water and seasonings to taste and consistency desired.
*Variation: Add a tomato or avocado while blending to make a salad dressing or spread for a sandwich.

SALADS AND DRESSINGS

MUSTARD
Reprinted from *The Country Life Natural Foods Cookbook*
Yield: 1 cup

What You Need

3/4 cup lemon juice
1/4 - 1/2 t salt
1/3 cup oil

1/4 cup soy flour
1 1/2 - 2 t turmeric or paprika
2 T garlic cloves, chopped

What You Do

1. Blend all ingredients well in blender, except oil and garlic.
2. Cook over medium heat, stirring constantly until thick. Cool.
3. Return to blender. While blending add garlic. Pour oil in slowly.

CATSUP
Yield: 1 cup

What You Need

1 cup tomato paste
2 T lemon juice
1/2 t basil
some water

1 t onion powder
1/2 t salt
1/2 t garlic powder
2-4 t honey (optional)

1. Mix all ingredients. Add water to desired consistency.

GAMASIO
Yield: 1 cup

What You Need

1 cup sesame seeds

1/4 to 1/2 t salt (to taste)

What You Do

1. Stirring constantly, roast seeds over medium heat in a dry skillet.
2. When seeds begin to pop, turn the heat off. Cool.
3. Add salt and blend to meal in your blender.

SALADS AND DRESSINGS

PESTO
Yield: 1 cup

What You Need

1/2 cup water
1 cup fresh sweet basil

1/2 cup olive oil
8 cloves of garlic

What You Do

1. Blend all ingredients in a blender. Add more or less garlic and basil to taste.
2. Store in a glass jar in your refrigerator.
3. Use on spaghetti, salads, soups, or to make garlic bread.

Sprouting

The Bible describes the attributes of the noble and virtuous woman in Proverbs 31. She brings her family good all the days of her life. She rises while it is still dark and provides food for her family as she watches over the affairs of her household. One of the most healthful foods that a woman can offer are sprouts. There are many reasons why sprouts are a good food. Sprouts are energizing, economical, ecological, educational, and easy to grow. In his search for a complete food, Dr. Clive Mckay, a nutritionist from Cornell University, asked for "a vegetable that will grow in any climate, rivals meat in nutritional value, matures in 3 to 5 days, may be planted any day of the year, requires neither soil nor sunshine and rivals tomatoes in vitamin C." The vegetable that fulfills all these requirements is soybean sprouts, but any sproutable seeds display the same general characteristics. It is true that sprouting does involve a certain amount of energy, time and space, but the results well outweigh the effort involved.

So much of the food that we eat today is either dead or dying, or we kill the nutrients by overcooking. This is not so with sprouts. They are alive and rich in the elements that build cells. Even as you are chewing raw sprouts, they are still growing.

Sprouting improves the quality, quantity and availability of a seed's nutritional makeup. During the growing process the protein in sprouts becomes converted into amino acids, which usually occur after food has been chewed and has traveled into the digestive tract. The lysine, one of the eight essential amino acids in wheat, rye and buckwheat, increases 2.4 to 5.7 times during the sprouting process. Mung beans increase in protein 16.6% to 18.25% in six days as a result of sprouting. Sprouts are low in fat because the sprouting process converts fat into carbohydrates. One cup of mung bean sprouts amounts to just 30 calories - high nutrition and low calories. The carbohydrate content of sprouts are converted to simple sugars; thus sprouts are a quick energy food because digestion has been accelerated during their growing period.

Studies show that sprouting increases the vitamin content by 100% to 1,500%. Beans and sunflower seeds, when sprouted, develop levels of vitamin C which are absent in the unsprouted seed. Alfalfa sprouts contain the entire B complex vitamins and are a good source of vitamins A, C, D, and E. The mineral content of alfalfa sprouts is high in calcium, magnesium, aluminum, sodium, sulfur, potassium, silicon, chlorine, and phosphorous.

The energy of any given plant is stored in its seed for the future growth of the new plants. A sprout is the beginning of this explosive reaction as the seed's water content increases from 12% to 95% during the soaking and rinsing of the sprouts. The potential energy and nutrients that would eventually spread throughout the entire plant are concentrated in the seed and then the sprout. So you can understand why a sprout is such a powerhouse of nutrition. Sprouts are economical. One pound of alfalfa seeds explodes into 6 to 8 pounds of sprouts. Three tablespoons of alfalfa seeds will fill up a two-quart canning jar with sprouts in six days. At $2.60 per pound, alfalfa seeds are a bargain at 11 cents for four ounces of sprouts. Mung beans multiply eight times when sprouted. At 69 cents a pound, mung bean sprouts cost 2 cents for 4 ounces. Sprouts save fuel because sprouted beans cook in half the time. Sprouting beans also helps beans loose their objectionable flatulent qualities.

Sprouts are ecological. There is no waste with sprouts. There are no wilted leaves to discard with crisp alfalfa sprouts. The water that you soak and rinse the seeds with can be recycled to water your houseplants. You can purchase mung bean sprouts in the grocery store, or grow your own and get the benefit of free chlorophyll from exposing your sprouts to the sun.

Sprouts are educational. The ABC of education is agriculture. After you start to sprout, the fun and fascination of sprouting will motivate you to experiment with a variety of seeds and methods. Sprouts are never boring because they are ever in the state of growth and change. Sprouting is an adventure for children and adults, so the family that sprouts together, grows together.

Researchers and scientists have been experimenting with sprouts since World War I. The British used sprouted peas and lentils to rid their troops of scurvy while in Mesopotamia. Dr. Santos of the Philippines used sprouted mung beans as the only source of the B-complex vitamins and cured patients with beri-beri. Dr. Tsuneo Kada, a mutation specialist at the National Institute of Genetics in Japan, has done extensive experimentation with bean and vegetable sprouts which have demonstrated the ability to inactivate cancer-causing substances in the human body. Other research has been one with sprouting grains for animal feed. Dairy farmers increase their milk output 10% to 20% by using sprouted oats. From the U.S. to Scotland to England to India, scientists are experimenting with sprouts and affirming their amazing nutritive and healing qualities.

Sprouting is a simple procedure, with the output outweighing the input. Some of the best, and easiest sproutable, include alfalfa and sunflower seeds, both of which are best eaten raw. Mung beans, lentils, garbanzos, wheat, and rye are best steamed before eating. The main point to remember when sprouting is to have good drainage. Rinse your sprouts with warm water, as cold water will retard growth. Storage of the mature sprouts in your refrigerator lengthens the life of the sprouts up to a week. Be sure not to let your refrigerated sprouts sit in water in their storage container or they will rot. You can sprout in a one or two quart wide-mouthed canning jar with nylon screening and a canning jar lid as a cover, or you can use cheesecloth or a nylon stocking and a rubber band as a cover. Trays, wet towels and colanders have been used as sprouting devices. You can even sprout in perforated plastic bags placed within another plastic bag for traveling or camping purposes.

The uses of sprouts are as varied as the number of seeds which are sproutable. They are good in salads and sandwiches. One or two day- old sunflower sprouts make for a delicious milk substitute when blended in the blender. Use 1 cup of sprouts to 3 cups of water, plus a pinch of salt, 2 to 3 tablespoons of sweetener, and a banana or coconut, or 3 tablespoons of carob powder, as optional taste enhancers. Bean sprouts are good steamed over rice, in soup, gravies, and burgers. The grain sprouts make for great cooked cereal for breakfast.

SALADS AND DRESSINGS

If you have never discovered sprouts, or if you are a backslidden sprouter, begin today making sprouting a habit.

References:

1. Albright, Nancy, "Sprouting Common Beans", *Organic Gardening and Farming*, Dec. 1975, pp. 87 - 88.
2. Elwood, Catharyn, *Feel Like a Million*, Devin-Adair, 1956.
3. Folkenberg, Gloria, "Eat a Live Thing", *Guide*, Jan. 22,1975, p.20.
4. Goulart, Frances, "Sprouts For Sport", *Vegetarian Times*, No. 26, pp. 44 - 45.
5. Ruttle, Jack, "Hassle Free Sprouting", *Organic Gardening and Farming*, Dec. 1975, pp. 125 - 127.
6. Walley, J. Zane, "A Garden in Your Pack", *Wilderness Camping Magazine*, 1597 Union St., Schenectady, NY 12309.
7. Weintraub, Sue, *Growing Sprouts for Good Eating*, Hippocrates Health Institute, 25 Exeter St., Boston, MA 02116.

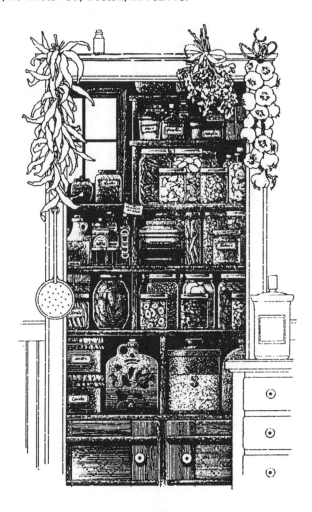

SUGARLESS DESSERTS

Sugarless Desserts

SUGARLESS DESSERTS

SUGARLESS DESSERTS

Re-evaluating Sugar

When you re-evaluate the use refined sugars from your food choices you may be loosing out on something. In order to achieve the greatest loss, you might consider only occasionally using honey, real maple syrup, barley malt, or molasses. You may loose out on obesity, tooth decay, diabetes, hypoglycemia, or constipation.

For 16 years my teenage son had been raised on a vegetarian diet without white sugars, and with limited amounts of honey and real maple syrup. Joshua has not had any cavities in his baby or adult teeth. His 13-year-old sister, Amber, and his 11-year-old brother, Noah, have been vegetarians from birth, and they do not have any cavities either. When the children were younger I said no to the bank teller, the gas station attendant, and the hardware store saleswomen when they asked if my children might have lollipops. Yes, they lost out on what has become an all too common part of American life - a worn out pancreas or depressed adrenals. Their loss is their gain. Today as the children make their own choices they have the advantage of the knowledge of the positive and negative sides of refined sugars. They also have the knowledge of the protection that regular tooth brushing and flossing give against cavities.

Something better is the watchword. Carob-covered BANANA POPSICLES and CHAMPION JUICER BANANA ICE CREAM replace high sugar dairy ice cream. Fresh fruits, carob balls and other homemade treats replace high sugar/high fat processed desserts. Watermelon is a summer staple at our house. We look forward to pomegranate, persimmon and apple season in the fall. There are numerous ways to use apples as treats. A few possibilities are DRIED APPLES, APPLE LEATHER, apple crisp, APPLE FLAT CAKE, APPLE BUTTER, and APPLE-DATE PIE. Fall is also chestnut time when you can enjoy the good taste of roasted chestnuts.

Winter brings a variety of oranges. January and February can be cheered up by a fresh pineapple or two to chase away cabin fever. Make it a point to inventory and stretch out your frozen summer berries, canned fruits and sauces, and dried fruits and leathers so that there will be enough for the later winter months. Make FRUIT SOUP as a late winter treat.

Spring mangoes tide us over before the summer flood of fresh fruit. Strawberries and cherries are looked forward to in June. Take your children to the orchard and berry patch. Grow your own garden and enjoy wholesome and healthful recreation.

SUGARLESS DESSERTS

Eat your food in its most natural state. Foster in yourself and your children an appreciation of the wholeness of natural foods. Look forward to fruits and vegetables in season. Make note daily, and remark as to the favor that God showers us with in the form of such luscious and appealing foods.

SUN BARS

Reprinted from *Uprisings: The Whole Grain Bakers' Book*
Yield: 12 pieces

What You Need

1 1/2 cup chopped dates
6 T barley malt
1 T vanilla
1 T water

2 1/4 cups sunflower seeds or
   halved almonds
1/4 cup peanut butter, tahini, or
   almond butter

What You Do

1. Blend seeds in blender to make a rough meal.
2. Mix all ingredients together. It will be quite gooey.
3. Press the mixture evenly into a well oiled 8 x 8 pan.
4. Bake at 350° for 20 minutes. The bottom will brown lightly.
5. Remove from oven and score into squares.
6. The bars will be soft when removed. Let them cool to room temperature and they will harden and become chewy.

*Variation: Eliminate barley malt and increase dates to 2 cups.

SUGARLESS DESSERTS

SESAME FINGERS
Adapted from *Ten Talents*
Yield: 30 rectangular pieces

What You Need

1 1/4 cup coconut
1/2 cup honey
1 T vanilla
1 T grated orange peel
1 T arrowroot

2 1/2 cups sesame seeds
1/2 cup DATE BUTTER
1/2 cup peanut butter, tahini, or
  almond butter
1/4 t salt (optional)

What You Do

1. Mix all ingredients.Spread evenly on an oiled cookie sheet.
2. Bake at 300° for 20 minutes. Will get crisp as cools. Cut.
*Variation: For crisper bars, blend 1/2 cup sunflower seeds and lessen sesame seeds by 1/2 cup.

RICE-OAT BARLEY BARS
Yield: 24 bars

What You Need

1 1/2 cups quick oats
1/2 cup coconut
1/2 t salt
1/2 cup raisins
3/4 cup barley malt
2 T arrowroot

1 1/2 cups rice flour
1/2 cup chopped pecans or
  walnuts
1/2 cup apple juice concentrate
1/4 cup oil or nut butter

What You Do

1. Mix dry and wet ingredients separately then combine.
2. Spoon onto oiled cookie sheet.
3. Place wax paper on top and roll evenly and smoothly with rolling pin.
4. Bake for 20 minutes at 350°.
5. Turn off heat and leave for 5 minutes.
6. Take out and score into squares while hot.

APPLE FLAT CAKE
Reprinted from *It's Your World Vegetarian Cookbook*
Yield: 24 squares

What You Need

2 cups rolled oats
2 T oil (optional)
1 T vanilla
1/4 cup raisins

1 1/2 cups apple juice
1/2 t salt
3 cups shredded apples
1/2 cup sunflower seeds
    or poppy seeds

What You Do

1. First, mix oats, salt and oil. Stir in remaining items.
2. Pour into oiled 10 x 15 baking pan.
3. Sprinkle top with poppy seeds.
4. Press down lightly and bake at 350° for 45 minutes.
5. Remove from oven and cut into squares.

TAHINI RAISIN OAT COOKIES
Reprinted from *Uprisings: The Whole Grain Bakers Book*
Yield: 24 cookies

What You Need

1 cup tahini
3/4 cup sunflower seed
1 cup raisins

3/4 cup honey
2 1/4 cup rolled oats
1/4 cup fruit juice

What You Do

1. Soak raisins in hot water.
2. Mix tahini and honey.
3. Add sunflower seeds and oats. Mix.
4. Drain and add raisins and fruit juice. Mix.
5. Drop by tablespoon on an oiled cookie sheet. Press with a wet fork to make round cookies.
6. Bake at 350° 15-20 minutes until bottoms become light brown.

CREATIVE OATMEAL COOKIES
Yield: 24 cookies

What You Need

2 cups quick oats
1/2 cup dried coconut
1/4 cup raisins or dates
1/2 cup nut butter
   or 1/2 cup tahini
1/2 cup unsweetened juice
   or applesauce
1/2 t salt

1/4-1/2 cup sweetener
1/4 cup carob chips,
   unsweetened
3 T arrowroot
1 cup cooked oatmeal
1 ripe banana or 1/2 cup or
   grated apple

What You Do

1. Mix oats, coconut, carob drops, raisins, salt and arrowroot in a mixing bowl. Then add cooked oatmeal.
2. Blend juice, banana, sweetener, and nut butter and add to dry ingredients. Mix well.
3. Let mixture sit for 15 minutes or until oats absorb the liquid.
4. If mixture is to runny, add more quick oats.
5. Spoon mixture onto 2 well oiled cookie sheets, using 2 T per cookie.
6. Bake at 350° for 30 minutes, until golden brown.
7. Let cookies cool before attempting to remove them from the cookie sheets.

*Variation: Oil only 1 cookie sheet and spread batter out evenly. Bake 35-40 minutes. After baking and cooling, cut into 24 bars.

COCONUT-TOFU MACAROONS
Yield: 36 small macaroons

What You Need

1/2 lb. firm tofu
3 T honey
1 T arrowroot
1 t almond extract (optional)

1/4 cup pineapple juice
2 T vanilla
2 cups dried coconut
1/2 t salt

What You Do

1. Mix arrowroot, coconut and salt in a bowl.
2. Blend smooth remaining ingredients. Mix all ingredients.
3. Place level teaspoon fulls on an oiled cookie sheet. Shape into mounds or leave a peak on top. Bake at 350° for 15 minutes.
4. Let cool for ten minutes on cookie sheet before removing.
*Variation: With your thumb make a depression in the macaroons and, after cooking, fill with a sugarless jam. Polander and Sorrell Ridge are two brands of sugar-less jams.

CAROB-FUDGE MACAROONS
Yield: 48 small macaroons

What You Need

1/2 lb. firm tofu
1/2 cup DATE BUTTER
2 T vanilla
1 T arrowroot

1/4 cup pineapple juice
2 cups coconut
1/4 cup carob powder
1/2 t salt
1 t almond extract (optional)

What You Do

1. Mix coconut, arrowroot, carob and salt in a bowl.
2. Blend smooth remaining ingredients.
3. Mix together the tofu mixture and carob mixture.
4. Oil two cookie sheets. Drop by teaspoons full. Shape.
5. Cook at 350° for 20 minutes.
6. Let macaroons cool ten minutes before removing.

RICE COOKIES
Yield: 15 cookies

What You Need

1 cup rice flour
1/2 cup coconut
1/2 cup walnuts, chopped
2 T honey
pinch salt

1 cup almond meal
1 cup grated carrot
1/2 lb. tofu
1/4 cup pineapple juice

What You Do

1. To make almond meal, blend 1 cup of almonds in a dry blender.
2. Mix rice flour, almond meal, coconut and salt in a bowl.
3. Combine carrots and walnuts, and add to flour mixture.
4. Blend honey, tofu and juice and add to dry ingredients.
5. Mix well. Spoon by tablespoons onto oiled cookie sheet.
6. Bake at 350° for 15 to 20 minutes. Watch for browning.

*Variation: Substitute applesauce for carrots, and raisins or dates for walnuts, and apple juice for pineapple juice.

GRAINLESS APPLE CRISP
Yield: servings for 6

What You Need

3 lbs. apples, sliced
1/2 cup sunflower seeds
1/2 cup sesame seeds
1 t coriander
1/2 t salt

1/2 cup raisins
1 cup coconut
1/2 cup barley malt (optional)
1 cup RAISIN BUTTER or DATE BUTTER

What You Do

1. Fill 8x8 with apple slices. Sprinkle with raisins and coriander.
2. Grind seeds in blender to make a meal. Stir in coconut.
3. Mix remaining items then mix all together. Should be moist but crumbly. Crumble over apples. Bake at 350° for 30-45 minutes. Serve hot or cold. May top with ALMOND CREAM.

RICE PUDDING
Yield: serves 4

What You Need

3 cups cooked brown rice
  or millet
1/2 cup raisins

1/2 cup almonds
1/2 to 1 cup pineapple juice
1/4 cup coconut

What You Do

1. Blend almonds and 1/2 cup pineapple juice in your blender until creamy. Add more juice, if necessary, to make cream pourable.
2. Mix rice, raisins and almond cream in a bowl. Sprinkle top with coconut. Chill or serve immediately.

*Variation: Fold in 1/2 cup of drained crushed pineapple before serving.

TOFU CHEESECAKE
Yield: serves 8

What You Need

1 cup oats or granola
2 1/4 lbs. tofu
1/4 cup tahini
3 T lemon juice
1 t coriander

1 T vegetable oil
3/4 t salt
1 cup honey or barley malt or
  maple syrup
1 T vanilla

What You Do

1. Mix oats, salt, honey, oil and 1/4# tofu. Press into 10" oiled pie plate. Blend remaining ingredients in food processor (blender can be used by not blending all filling at once.)
2. Pour filling in pie crust and bake at 350° for 40 minutes. Should be firm on top and slightly brown. Cool. Add topping.

TOPPING: 3 cups strawberries, blueberries, or cherries, 1/2 cup pineapple juice, 2 T arrowroot. Cook juice and arrowroot until clear, stirring. Cool and add fruit.

*Variation: Eliminate crust. Pour filling directly into oiled pie pan.

SUGARLESS DESSERTS

QUICK AND EASY TOFU CHEESE CAKE
Reprinted from *Cooking with Natural Foods*
Yield: 1 cake

What You Need

2 cups tofu
1 T vanilla
2 T arrowroot
1 banana

1 T lemon juice
20 oz. can crushed pineapple
pinch salt

What You Do

1. Blend all ingredients in your blender.
2. Place in oiled pie plate and bake at 350° for 30-35 minutes.

LEMON CUSTARD
Adapted from Beverly Sills' recipe in
Celebrity Chefs Recipes
Yield: five 1/2-cup servings

What You Need

10 dried sulphured
  apricots
1/2 lb. soft or silken tofu
1/3 cup fresh squeezed
  lemon juice

2 1/2 cups pineapple juice
2 T Emes Plain Kosher Gel or
  1/4 cup Agar flakes
1 T lemon rind
1 - 2 T honey (optional)

What You Do

1. In a pot simmer 1/2 cup pineapple juice and the dried apricots to soften the apricots.
2. In another pot combine 2 cups pineapple juice and 2 T Emes gelatin and bring to boil and then turn off immediately.
3. Let both pots cool, then place contents of both in a blender, and add the tofu, lemon juice, lemon rind and honey to taste. Blend until creamy.
4. Pour into custard cups and refrigerate at least 2 hours.
5. Before serving, you can top with crushed pineapple and a sprig of fresh mint.

SUGARLESS DESSERTS

STRAWBERRY MOUSSE
Adapted from *Nasoya Tofu Cookbook*
Yield: serves 5

What You Need

2 cups white grape juice
1/2 lb. silken tofu
3 cups frozen or fresh strawberries

2 T Emes plain kosher gel or 2 T
    agar flakes

What You Do

1. In a saucepan, bring to boil, and immediately turn off and cool: white grape juice, Emes vegetarian gel, or agar flakes.
2. In a blender, blend juice, tofu, and frozen or fresh strawberries.
3. Pour into a deep dish glass pie plate.
4. Cover with plastic wrap and refrigerate at least 4 hours, until the mixture solidifies.

PEACH MOUSSE
Yield: 8 cups

What You Need

2 cups white grape juice
2 T Emes Plain Kosher Gel
1 banana
2 T honey

12 dried apricots
1/2 lb. soft or silken tofu
3-4 cups fresh or frozen
    peaches

What You Do

1. In a saucepan bring to boil grape juice, apricots and gelatin. Stir to dissolve gelatin.
2. Turn off and let cool.
3. When cool blend with rest of ingredients in your blender.
4. Pour into an attractive serving bowl or mold. Refrigerate.
5. Will set as does Jell-O.

SUGARLESS DESSERTS

TOFU VANILLA PUDDING
Yield: serves 4

What You Need

1 lb. silken tofu
1 T vanilla
1/4 t salt

1/3 to 1/2 cup maple syrup or
   honey
2 T oil

What You Do

1. Blend all ingredients.
2. Divide into four 1/2 cup servings. Chill.
3. Before serving, add chopped strawberries, blueberries or raspberries.

TAPIOCA PUDDING
Yield: serves two

What You Need

1/4 lb. tofu
1/4 cup cashews
1/4 t salt
1 T vanilla

1/3 cup instant tapioca
2 cup water
1/4 cup sweetener

What You Do

1. Blend until creamy tofu, cashews, 1 cup water, salt, and vanilla.
2. Add 1 more cup water and blend.
3. In saucepan put milk from blender and tapioca.
4. Heat to boil, stirring constantly.
5. Turn down and simmer 10 minutes.
6. Add 1/4 cup sweetener. Optional: 1/4 cup raisins.
7. Serve hot or chill and serve with sliced bananas.

MANGO BANANA PUDDING
Yield: serves 2-4

What You Need

2 mangoes   2 bananas

What You Do

1. Put the flesh of mangoes and bananas in your blender and blend until creamy. Should be rather thick.
2. Eat the cream as it is, or chill or freeze it. Makes a good dip for crackers.

BARLEY PIE CRUST
Yields one 9" pie crust

What You Need

1/2 cup almond butter   1/2 cup water
1 cup barley flour   1/4 t salt

What You Do

1. Mix almond butter, barley flour, and salt with fork.
2. Add water. Mix into ball. Roll out between wax paper.
3. Place in 9" oiled pie shell. Bake 15-20 minutes at 350°.

BARLEY OAT PIE CRUST
Yield: one 9" pie crust

What You Need

1 cup barley flour   1 cup oat flour (blend oats)
1/3 cup oil   1/3 cup water
1/4 t salt

What You Do

1. Mix flour and salt. Stir in oil. Add water, mix into ball.
2. Roll out between wax paper. Bake in 9 inch pie shell at 350° for 15-20 minutes.

CAROB PUDDING OR PIE FILLING
Yield: pudding for 8

What You Need

4 cups milk (CASHEW or soy)
1 1/2 t Pero or Cafix
1/2 t salt
1/2 cup honey or DATE
  BUTTER

1/4 cup coconut
4-6 T carob powder
1 t vanilla
1/2 cup arrowroot

What You Do

1. Blend all ingredients in your blender.
2. Lightly boil stirring constantly until thick.
3. Make a crustless pie by filling a pie plate or fill individual cups. May sprinkle with extra coconut.
4. Cover with plastic wrap to prevent hard film from forming.
5. You may slice bananas, cover the bottom of the pieplate, and pour the pudding on top. Top with ALMOND CREAM or TOFU WHIPPED CREAM.

PECAN PIE FILLING
Adapted from *Brother Ron's Friendly Foods Cookbook*
Yield: one 9" pie shell

What You Need

3 1/2 cups pecans
1/4 cup rice syrup
1 t vanilla extract

1 cup barley malt
1 T arrowroot

What You Do

1. Roast pecans at 250° for 20 minutes. Cool.
2. Blend in blender or food processor to make meal.
3. Mix remaining ingredients.
4. Add pecan meal and mix well. Will be thick and gooey.
5. Spoon into uncooked pie shell or make without a crust.
6. Arrange 1/2 cup whole pecans in decorative circle on top.
7. Bake at 350° for 30 minutes.

SHREDDED APPLE PIE
Yield: serves 6

What You Need

2 cups rolled oats
1/4 cup tapioca
1/4 t salt

2 cups pineapple or apple juice
1 cup applesauce
2 cups shredded raw apples

What You Do

1. Make crust by mixing oats, salt and applesauce.
2. Press into an oiled 8" pie pan. Bake at 350° for 35 minutes.
3. Make filling by combining juice and tapioca in a saucepan. Let set for five minutes. Bring to boil, stirring constantly.
4. Lower heat and cook until tapioca becomes clear.
5. Set aside and let cool.
6. Add shredded apples and mix well.
7. Pour in pie shell and chill. Sprinkle top with coconut.

APPLE PIE FILLING
Yield: filling for one pie

What You Need

7 cups sliced apples
1 T orange juice concentrate
1 t coriander

1 cup pineapple juice
1 cup chopped dates

What You Do

1. In a saucepan, simmer the dates, pineapple juice, apples, and coriander for 3-5 minutes until dates soften.
2. Place in unbaked pie shell.
3. Cover with top crust, flute edges, and cut slits on top.
4. Bake at 350° for 45 minutes or until flute-edges are solid but not hard.
5. To glaze the pie, brush with orange juice concentrate when pie comes out of the oven.
6. For crustless dessert, fill pudding dishes with softened apple mixture, chill and top with ALMOND CREAM.

CRUSTLESS SQUASH PIE
Yield: 9" pastry pie pan

What You Need

2 cups cooked squash
1 cup softened dates
6 T arrowroot
1/2 t salt
1 cup coconut or ALMOND CREAM

2 cups NUT or soy MILK
2 T molasses
1 t vanilla
2 t coriander

What You Do

1. Soften dates by simmering with nut milk on a low heat for 3 to .5 minutes.
2. Blend all ingredients well. Use a food processor if available, or divide ingredients and use your blender.
3. Pour into a deep 9" pie pan.
4. Bake at 450° for 10 minutes.
5. Lower temperature to 350° for 35 minutes until pie has set.
6. Top with cream.

ALMOND CREAM
Yield: 1 1/2 to 2 cups

What You Need

1 1/2 cups pineapple
  juice

1 cup almonds or cashews
a pinch of salt

What You Do

1. In a dry blender blend almonds or cashews to meal.
2. Add juice and salt and blend until creamy.
3. Chill. Will thicken when refrigerated.

SUGARLESS DESSERTS

TOFU WHIPPED CREAM
Yield: 1 1/2 cups

What You Need

1 cup soft or silken tofu
1/4 cup pineapple juice
2 T honey
1/2 cup coconut or Soyagen

1/4 t salt
1 t vanilla
1 T lemon juice (optional)

What You Do

1. Blend smooth all ingredients.
2. Refrigerate. Stores 3-4 days.

FRUIT KABOBS or FRUIT SALAD ON-A-STICK

What You Need

whole strawberries
apple chunks
pineapple chunks

melon chunks
pitted cherries
seedless grapes

What You Do

1. Purchase individual disposable, double-pointed wooden Kabob sticks at a hardware store or cooking supply store.
2. Arrange the fruit on the kabob sticks.

PINEAPPLE BUTTERFLY
Yield: 1 butterfly for one

What You Need

1 whole pineapple ring
1 apricot

1/8 cup raisins
1 date

What You Do

1. Cut the pineapple in half to make the wings. Put a date in the middle for the abdomen. Top the pineapple with raisins. Slice apricot in thin strips and place as the antennae.

HOLIDAY CANDLE
Yield: 1 candle for one

What You Need

1 pineapple ring   1/2 banana
1 strawberry or cherry

What You Do

1. Put the whole pineapple ring on a plate.
2. Stand 1/2 peeled banana in the center of the pineapple ring.
3. Top with strawberry or cherry for the flame.

TAPIOCA FRUIT SALAD
Reprinted from *The Joy of Cooking Naturally*
Yield: serves 4 to 6

What You Need

2 cups sliced peaches   1 cup sliced strawberries
2 bananas sliced   1 cup blueberries
1 1/2 cups water   2 T quick cooking tapioca
6 oz. or 3/4 cup orange juice concentrate

What You Do

1. Soak tapioca in water for 15 minutes.
2. Cook over medium heat, stirring constantly until gently boiling and tapioca is clear.
3. Remove from heat. Stir in orange juice concentrate.
4. Pour into serving bowl and refrigerate.
5. When ready to serve, fold in sliced peaches, blueberries, sliced strawberries, and bananas.

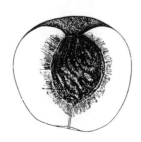

BASIC FRUIT GEL
Yield: 4 cups

What You Need

3 T Emes Plain Kosher
  Gelatin or 2 T powdered
  agar or 4 T flaked agar
  or 2 sticks agar

4 cups any fruit juice
2 cups chopped fruit of your
  choice

What You Do

1. Stir gelatin into 1 cup of juice.
2. Bring to boil.
3. Remove from stove and pour in 3 cups of juice.
4. Add chopped fruit of your choice.
5. Pour into a mold or bowl and chill, covered, 5-8 hours.
6. Gelatin will become firm in your refrigerator.

PINA-COLADA GEL
Yield: 4 cups

What You Need

2 T Emes Plain Kosher
  Gelatin

4 cups pina colada juice
1 cup cubed pineapple

What You Do

1. Bring to boil gelatin and 1 cup juice.
2. Take off stove and add remaining ingredients.
3. Pour into mold or bowl and refrigerate until firm.

CRANBERRY-PINEAPPLE SAUCE
Yield: 3 cups

What You Need

1 lb. fresh cranberries
1/2 cup honey
1/2 cup chopped walnuts

3-6 orhnges, peeled
1-16 oz can crushed
  pineapple

What You Do

1. Grind fresh cranberries and peeled oranges in a food grinder.
2. Add pineapple, chopped walnuts and honey to taste.
3. Chill before serving.
*Variation: Substitute 3 T orange juice concentrate for whole oranges. Blend cranberries and orange juice in blender. Or drain crushed pineapple and heat juice with 2 T Emes gelatin or agar and add to blender to make molded sauce.

Ice Creams

PINEAPPLE PARSLEY SHERBET
Yield: 3 cups

What You Need

2 cups crushed pineapple or 2 cups pineapple juice
2 handfuls fresh parsley   1 banana (optional)

What You Do

1. Blend all smooth until frosty and green.
2. Freeze in an ice tray or individual cups or
   popsicle molds or drink immediately.

BANANA POPSICLES

Reprinted from *The Country Life Natural Foods Cookbook*
Yield: 8 Popsicles

What You Need

4 bananas
1 cup ground coconut
8 popsicle sticks
1 cup chopped nuts (optional)

CAROB PEANUT BUTTER
  FROSTING
2 cups DATE BUTTER
  (optional)

What You Do

1. Peel four bananas and then cut them in half and place on popsicle sticks.
2. Cover each with CAROB PEANUT BUTTER FROSTING or plain DATE BUTTER.
3. Roll in coconut or chopped nuts and place on a plate, cover loosely with plastic wrap and freeze.

CAROB PEANUT BUTTER FROSTING

Reprinted from *The Country Life Natural Foods Cookbook*
Yield: enough to cover 8 Popsicles

What You Need

3/4 cup water
1/2 cup peanut butter
1 t vanilla

1/4-1/2 cup carob powder
1/2 cup DATE BUTTER

What You Do

1. Heat water and carob in a saucepan until thick.
2. Remove from heat. Stir in rest of ingredients and mix well.

PEACH ICE CREAM
Reprinted from *The Country Life Natural Foods Cookbook*
Yield: 5 cups

What You Need

1 cup cashew nuts or
   sunflower seeds
1/4 cup honey
3 T orange juice concentrate

2 1/2 cup peach liquid or water
2 cups peach halves
   (unsugared)

What You Do

1. Blend all ingredients until smooth.
2. You may add pieces of fresh fruit at this point.
3. Pour into an 8 x 8 pan or freezer trays and freeze.
4. Thaw slightly before serving.

STRAWBERRY ICE
Yield:3 cups

What You Need

1 3/4 cups orange juice
3 pints strawberries
1/4 cup honey or to taste

1/4 cup lemon juice
1/8 t salt

What You Do

1. Blend all ingredients. Pour into 9 x 13 pan or ice cube trays.
3. Cover with plastic and freeze.

QUICK COOLING TREAT

1. Place peeled bananas in plastic bags and freeze. You can eat them as a frozen dessert. A frozen banana is a cooling alternative to any frozen dairy product.
2, Place unopened 20 ounce can of unsweetened pineapple chunks in freezer. Once frozen remove and defrost 1/2 hour. Remove top and bottom of the can and push contents into blender. Blend and serve immediately as pineapple sherbet. Stem seedless grapes, freeze. Delicious frozen treat.

THE CHAMPION JUICER - ICE CREAM MAKER

Take frozen peeled bananas and put them through a Champion Juicer. The end product is creamy and delicious; you will think you are eating a Carvel or Dairy Queen, but it is pure banana. You can also freeze strawberries, peaches, or any fruit and put them through in the same manner, or mix fruits together to make interesting combinations. Banana blueberry ice cream. Sound good? It is. A food processor can be used to make frozen fruit creamy, but it does not work as well as the Champion Juicer.

CHAMPION JUICER BASIC PROCEDURE

The Champion Juicer is a homogenizer as well as a juicer. As a homogenizer the Champion Juicer produces creamy ice cream. You can purchase a Champion Juicer through Country Life Natural Foods, 15 Roxbury Street, Keene, New Hampshire 03431, or write Plastaket Manufacturing, 6220 East Highway 12, Lodi, California 95240. Or try your local health food store. Shop around for a good deal.

1. Mix ice cream ingredients in a large bowl.
2. Divide mixture into 2 or 3 portions. Blend a portion at a time in your blender or food processor. Re-mix ingredients after blending.
3. Pour mixture into ice cube trays with the center sections removed, cover with plastic and freeze.
4. After the mixture is frozen, usually overnight, remove from freezer and let stand at room temperature one half hour.
5. Cut the frozen ice cream mixture into strips that will fit into the juicer's hopper.
6. Use solid nylon fixture instead of juice screen. Run frozen strips through the juicer.
7. Serve immediately, or you can refreeze for later serving. The flavor of the carob is enhanced by time. I run the mix through the juicer an hour or two before serving and refreeze it and the consistency remains the same. If strawberry or maple walnut are frozen over night, or longer, they tend to get a bit icy.

ICE CREAM MACHINE PROCEDURE

1. Mix ingredients in a large bowl.
2. Divide mix into 2 or 3 portions and blend in your blender or
· food processor a portion at a time.
3. Mix the blended portions together.
4. Follow the directions for your ice cream machine.

SUGARLESS DESSERTS

TOFU-STRAWBERRY ICE CREAM
Yield: 10 cups

What You Need

1 1/2 lbs. tofu (soft)
1/2 cup honey
1/8 cup lemon juice
2 medium ripe bananas
1/4 t salt

2 cups nut or soy milk
2-16 ozs. strawberries (frozen
  or fresh)
2 T vanilla

What You Do

1. Make milk first. If using soy milk powder follow directions on package. Almond milk can be made by blending together 1/2 cup of almonds and 1 1/2 cups of water until creamy.
2. Mash bananas and tofu in a bowl.
3. Stir in remaining ingredients well. Follow basic procedure.

TOFU-MAPLE WALNUT ICE CREAM
Yield: 7 cups

What You Need

1 1/2 lbs. tofu (soft)
1 cup shelled walnuts
2 bananas
1/4 t salt

1/2 cup pure maple syrup
1 1/2 cups water
3 T vanilla

What You Do

1. Make walnut milk by blending 1/2 cup of walnuts and the water until creamy. Mash bananas and tofu in a bowl.
2. Stir in remaining ingredients, except 1/2 cup walnuts.
3. Follow basic procedure.
4. Before serving, chop remaining 1/2 cup of walnuts and mix into the ice cream.
*Variation: Substitute 1/2 cup of almonds for walnuts to make Maple Almond Ice Cream or use an ice cream scoop to make an ice cream ball, roll in dry coconut and serve as a snowball in foil baking cups.

CAROB-TOFU ICE CREAM
Yield: 1/2 gallon

What You Need

1 1/2 lbs. tofu (soft)
1/2 cup carob powder
2 large bananas
3 T vanilla
1/4 t salt

1 cup dates or raisins
1/2 cup almonds or sunflower
   seeds
1 1/2 cups water

What You Do

1. Blend smooth nuts or seeds with water.
2. Heat dates in this milk until dates soften. Cool.
3. Blend date and milk mixture in your blender.
4. Mash 2 bananas and tofu in a large bowl.
5. Stir in remaining ingredients.
6. Follow basic procedure.

MILLET-CAROB ICE CREAM
Reprinted from *Newstart Homestyle*
Yield: 1/2 gallon

What You Need

1 cup cooked millet (hot)
1 cup dates
1/2 cup carob powder
1 T vanilla

2 1/2 cups water
1/4 cup natural peanut butter
2 ripe bananas

What You Do

1. Soften dates in 1 cup of water by heating on stove. Let cool
   and blend in your blender. Empty.
2. Add 1 1/2 cup of water, millet, vanilla and peanut butter.
   Blend until smooth.
3. Add bananas and carob and blend. Mix all ingredients.
4. Follow basic procedures.

MARY ZUMBO'S RICE CREAM ICE CREAM
Yield: 6 to 7 cups

What You Need

1 cup dry brown rice
1 cup cashews or almonds
3 cups water
pinch salt

6 cups water
2 T Emes Plain Kosher Gelatin
1/2 cup honey
1-2 T vanilla

What You Do

1. Cook one cup brown rice in 3 cups water.
2. Put cooked rice through a Foley food mill to make 2 cups of rice cream. The husks of the rice should remain in the food mill.
3. Place remaining water in a saucepan. Stir in gelatin and bring to boil. Turn off immediately, remembering to stir to keep the gelatin from sticking. Cool.
4. Blend nuts with 1 cup of cooled water and Emes until mixture is creamy. Combine blended nuts with remaining 2 cups of Emes water plus additional water to equal one quart.
5. Add rice cream, honey, salt and vanilla and blend.
6. Follow the basic procedure.

Carob

Many think that changing your diet for health reasons is a sacrifice. Usually a questionable food or activity can be limited rather than eliminated. I present a challenge. Anything you find that is not healthy, but deceivingly appealing to the palate, can be replaced with something better that is naturally good tasting and healthy. "Something Better" is the watchword of education.

There are certain foods or chemicals in foods that should be eliminated to bring about a state of optimum health. Nicotine, caffeine, alcohol, and chocolate are several that come to mind. How can I classify chocolate with so-called legal drugs? Chocolate contains methylxanthines (rhymes with Ethel Francine) such as caffeine and theobromine which are habit-forming substances. The ingesting of methylxanthines results in central nervous system stimulation, sleeplessness, itching, depression, or anxiety.

Chocolate is one of the most common allergens. The natural bitterness of chocolate necessitates a high percentage of sugar to make it palatable. Do you experience a quick lift after eating chocolate, but also quick fatigue soon after? Chocolate is 52% fat. Are you concerned with your cholesterol level? The high fat content makes chocolate highly susceptible to rancidity; therefore processors compensate by including additives and texture agents in the finished product. Chocolate milk accounts for 90% of all milk sold in schools. A candy bar contains 78 milligrams of caffeine, which is half as much as a cup of coffee. With the negative information on chocolate, parents might want to re-evaluate the choices for their children and educate them. Chocolate has addictive qualities, so when you choose to stop you may experience withdrawal symptoms. But persist, for in 5 to 10 days your body will be cleansed.

Cocoa is a tree grown in tropical regions which produces pods that are cut and piled in heaps outside to ferment from 3 to 8 days. The piles become homes for insects and rodents. Aflatoxin, a cancer-producing agent from molds, can develop during the fermentation process. Fermentation is what develops the chocolate taste. The processing of chocolate is under such unsanitary conditions that the FDA has specifications for levels of insect and rodent contaminants allowed in chocolate sold on the retail market. For more information you can write to: FDA Guidelines and Compliance Branch, Bureau of Foods, 200 C Street SW, Washington, DC 20204.

SUGARLESS DESSERTS

The truth about chocolate sounds grim; but remember, "Something Better" is the watchword. Carob is an alternative to chocolate. CarŒb comes from a tree grown in the Middle East. The pods are dried and ground to produce carob powder. Classified as a legume, carob is 8% protein and 46% natural sugar. Carob is rich in B vitamins, calcium, magnesium, and potassium. The naturally sweet carob is a nutritional food as well. Carob has three times more calcium than chocolate, but contains one third the calories and seventeen times less fat. Statistics make carob a winner. Taste-wise, carob has its own unique flavor which can be appreciated by chocolate lovers for its nutritional value and absence of harmful stimulation. A word of caution: beware of processed carob confections which can be high in fat and sweeteners. Be a label reader. You can find carob powder at your local co-op or natural foods store and develop your own treats.

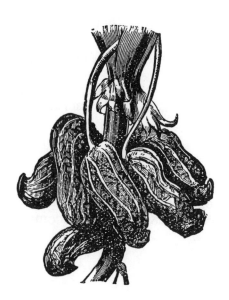

SUGARLESS DESSERTS

CAROB BALLS
Yield: 20 carob balls

What You Need

1/4 cup carob powder
1 cup peanut butter
1/4 cup coconut

2-4 T honey
1/4 cup sunflower seed

What You Do

1. Blend seeds to a meal in dry blender.
1. Mix all ingredients together well.
2. Roll mixture into small balls 1 1/2 inches in palm of hand.
3. If too dry, add more peanut butter or honey. If very mushy, add more meal.
4. Roll balls in coconut.
*Variation: Add walnuts and/or raisins.

CAROB SAUCE
Reprinted from *Ten Talents*
Yield: 1 1/2 cups

What You Need

1/4 cup carob powder
1 cup soy or nut milk
a pinch of salt

1/3 cup DATE BUTTER
1/2 t vanilla

What You Do

1. Lightly boil, stirring, as the mixture thickens.
2. Use on banana ice cream or waffles.
3. If you use CASHEW MILK, the taste becomes quite chocolaty.

WALNUT FUDGE SQUARES
Yield: 12 to 16 squares

What You Need

1/2 cup ground walnuts
1/2 cup tahini
1/4 cup DATE BUTTER
2 T water (optional)

1/2 cup chopped walnuts
1/4 cup honey
1/4 cup carob powder

What You Do

1. Mix ground walnuts, tahini, and honey.
2. Add carob and date butter.
3. Add chopped nuts.
4. Consistency should be moist, not too dry, but also not too sticky. Add water if too dry.
5. Lightly oil small square glass baking dish.
6. Spread mixture in dish to 1/4 inch thickness. Chill.
7. Cut into squares. Rich tasting.

CAROB HALVA
Yield: 10 to 15 balls

What You Need

1/2 cup tahini
1-2 T carob powder
1/4 cup honey

1/3 cup sunflower or sesame
   seed meal (blend in dry
   blender)

What You Do

1. Mix ingredients together well and roll into small balls about one inch in diameter, or shape into a mound to be sliced.
2. Refrigerate. It is also freezable.
*Variation: Mix all except carob and then mix carob lightly for a marble-like effect.

CAROB SHAKE
Yield: 1 1/2 cups

What You Need

1-2 bananas
2-4 T carob powder
1 cup water

1/2 cup cashews or almonds or
   sunflower seeds

What You Do

1. Blend nuts or seeds and water until creamy.
2. Add carob and bananas, depending on sweetness you desire and richness of carob you are using. Blend.
3. Add water to create desired consistency. Blend.
4. If you don't drink it all, place remainder in an ice cube tray or popsicle molds and make a carob fudgesicle.

PUFFED CEREAL BALLS
Reprinted from *Amazing Facts Something Better Cookbook*
Yield: about 20 balls

What You Need

2 T carob
1/2 cup warm water
1 cup finely shredded dried coconut

2 T honey
2 cups puffed rice or millet

What You Do

1. Mix carob and of warm water.
2. Add honey.
3. Stir in puffed rice and coconut.
4. Let stand 20 minutes.
5. Form mixture into balls. Refrigerate.
6. These balls will firm up during refrigeration.

PRESERVING NATURALLY

PRESERVING NATURALLY

"Now, He who supplies seed to the sower and bread for food, will supply and multiply your seed for sowing and increase the harvest of your righteousness." 2 Corinthians 9:10, NAS.

PEACH-APPLE PECTIN JAM
Adapted from *Organic Gardening*
Yield: 5 cups

What You Need

2 T lemon juice
1 cup sliced apples with skin

1/4-1/2 cup honey
4 cups fresh sliced peaches

What You Do

1. Grate or chop fine 1 cup apples with skin.
2. Simmer apples until soft.
3. Add remaining ingredients and simmer until mix thickens-this can take up to an hour. This jam is not as thick as regular jam, but will thicken some in the jar.
4. Blend in blender or process through a Foley Food Mill.
5. Process hot jam in hot jars and water bath 15 minutes.

PEACH-APPLE CONCENTRATE SAUCE
Adapted from *Organic Gardening*
Yield: 4 1/2 pints

What You Need

3 lbs. sliced fresh peaches with skin or about 12 med. peaches
6 oz. frozen apple juice concentrate

What You Do

1. In a pot, mash the peaches.
2. Add thawed apple concentrate.
3. Bring to boil, stir and simmer uncovered.
4. Will thicken in 30 to 45 minutes.
5. Press through sieve or food mill.
6. Process hot jam in hot jars and water bath 15 minutes.

PRESERVING NATURALLY

COLD PACK PEACHES OR PEARS
CANNED IN PINEAPPLE JUICE
Yield: 12 quarts

What You Need

20 lbs. peaches or 1 bushel   6-12 cups of water
1 46 fl. oz. can unsweetened pineapple juice (6 cups)
12 1-quart canning jars, lids and rings

What You Do

1. Bring 3 quarts of water to boil in a 4-quart pot.
2. Make a bag out of cheesecloth and put 6 peaches in the bag to dip into the boiling water for 30 seconds, then right into a sink of cold water. Remove the skins. Repeat until all peaches have had their skins removed.
3. Slice or halve the skinned peaches into a large bowl filled with 1 cup of pineapple juice and 3 cups of water.
4. Fill the canning jars with peaches from the bowl, pressing down lightly on peaches as you fill the jar.
5. When the jar is full to 1 inch from its top, fill in the rest with the pineapple juice water mixture.
6. Diluted juice proportion is 1 cup of juice to 3 cups of water. If you want a sweeter liquid, increase the amount of juice and decrease water proportionately.
7. Insert a knife carefully down the sides of jar to release any trapped air. Clean jar rim and put on clean lid and ring.
8. Process in a water bath for 15-20 minutes.
9. You can also can pear halves, using the same method, but it is not necessary to skin the pears.

APPLESAUCE

1. Cortlands make a sweet, pink sauce. Need no sweetener.
2. Mix Cortland, Red Delicious, and Ida Red for a good tasting unsweetened sauce.
3. Use pears to make a pear sauce - a pleasant change.
4. If you are allergic to the mold on fruit, peel your apples before saucing them, or you can soak your apples in 1 capful bleach to a sink of water for 10-15 minutes; then soak in clear water for the same time.

233

ORANGE PEEL

1. If possible, using unsprayed oranges is best.
2. Peel the skin off an orange or tangerine minus the white parts.
3. Dry on your wood stove, or in your oven at low heat, or even above your furnace.
4. Tangerine peels give off wonderful odors as they dry.
5. Dry until peel becomes crisp. Grind small amounts in blender.
6. Store in a glass air-tight container.
7. Use as a seasoning in APPLE CRISP or recipe of your choice.

DRIED APPLE RINGS
Yield: 6-8 rings

1. Peel and core the apple and slice into thick rings.
2. Make sure all seeds and bad spots have been removed.
3. Thread rings on string. Hang over hot wood stove or furnace.
4. Drying time depends on the heat source temperature.
5. Apple rings should be dry and pliable.

FRUIT LEATHER BASIC PROCEDURE

1. A dehydrator or oven with a gas pilot light is more energy-efficient than an electric stove set at 100° to 150° or warm.
2. A 2-cup recipe fills a 10x15 pan. A 3-cup fills a 12x17 pan.
3. Oil cookie sheets with lecithin or Pam spray .Or line with plastic wrap, leaving a 3-inch overhang on each end.
4. Blend mixture in food processor or blender. If using blender pre-mix ingredients and blend a portion at a time.
5. Pour mixture evenly 1/8 to 1/4" thick on cookie sheets.
6. Choose heat source. Electric oven takes 2-6 hours.
7. Cool when dry, peel off cookie sheet, and roll in wax paper to store. Does not have to be refrigerated.

PINEAPPLE LEATHER

What You Need

fresh pineapple or well drained can of pineapple
2 bananas

What You Do

1.Blend smooth. Follow FRUIT LEATHER PROCEDURE.

APPLE LEATHER

1. Peel and slice6-8 apples into small pieces and blend in blender. Simmer on stove without any added water.
2. Follow the FRUIT LEATHER BASIC PROCEDURE.

PEACH LEATHER

What You Need

3 cups peeled and   1 cup canned crushed pineapple
  sliced peaches   1/2 banana (optional)

1. Blend all ingredients. See FRUIT LEATHER PROCEDURE.
*Variation: Use just peaches.

PEAR LEATHER

What You Need

3 cups blended pears   1/2 banana
1 apple peeled and cut into chunks

What You Do

1. Pears have a high water content. Peel, slice and cut out cores. Mash enough pears to make 3 cups.
2. Blend all ingredients. See FRUIT LEATHER PROCEDURE.
*Variation: Eliminate apple and banana. Substitute 1/4 cup orange juice, 1 T orange juice concentrate and 1 cup dried apple.

DILLED FRESH ZUCCHINI
Reprinted from *Organic Gardening, Rodale Press*
Yield: 10-12 pints

What You Need

2 cups chopped onion   6 lbs. young fresh zucchini
1/4 cup dill seed   2 cups finely sliced celery
4 cups lemon juice   6 cloves of garlic
salt is optional

What You Do

1. Peel, seed, and slice zucchini lengthwise into strips 4" long and 1/4" thick.
2. Mix all vegetables in a large bowl and cover with ice.
3. Let stand at room temperature 3 hours.
4. Combine the dill seed and lemon juice and bring to boil.
5. Drain vegetables, add them to the lemon juice mixture, and bring to boil again.
6. Pack into hot pint jars, adding 1 clove of garlic per jar.
7. Cap and process 15 minutes in boiling water bath.

Additional Supports

SUPPORT and RESOURCES

The Home Medical Reference Library

Health information is readily available in books, magazines, newspapers, radio, TV and other videos. The problem is how to weed through all the information and determine what is truth and what will apply to your situation. With non-life-threatening medical problems it has made sense to me to first try natural remedies and simple treatments, which allow the body to mend itself, before risking the inevitable side effects of drugs. The priority is preventive medicine. Following the Eight Laws of Health will allow the body to fight unavoidable exposure to germs, and resist disease. The following is by no means an exhaustive list, but some suggestions of references I have used in successfully treating my family with natural remedies and simple treatments.

Before purchasing books, research at your local library. Utilize the children's sections as well, especially for references on human anatomy. Juvenile anatomy and physiology books have large illustrations and simple yet explicit explanations. Your local library and interlibrary loan services can help you review books before deciding if you want to purchase them. Health books are classified in the 600s: 610, Medical Science; 611, Human Anatomy; 614, Public Health; 616, Medicine; 641, Nutrition; 649, Parenting.

A. Self-care books strongly recommended to have in your home:
1. Austin, Phylis, Thrash, Agatha, MD, and Thrash, Calvin, MD, *Natural Remedies: A Manual*, Family Health Publications, Sunfield, MI 48890.
2. Austin, Phylis, Thrash, Agatha, MD, and Thrash, Calvin, MD, *More Natural Remedies*, Family Health Publications, Sunfield, MI 48890.
3. Dail, Charles, MD, and Thomas, Charles, PhD, *Simple Remedies for the Home*, Preventive Health Care and Education Center, 4027 W. George St., Banning, CA 92220.
4. Hansen, Richard, MD, *Get Well At Home*, Shiloh Medical Publications, Box 4070, Poland Springs, ME 04274.
5. Kloss, Jethro, *Back to Eden*, Woodbridge Publishing Company, PO Box 6189, Santa Barbara, CA 93111.
6. Peterson, Stella, RN, *Hydrotherapy in the Home*, Mountain Missionary Press, PO Box 807, Harrisville, NH 03450-0807.
7. Thrash, Agatha, MD, and Thrash, Calvin, MD, *Home Remedies: Hydrotherapy, Massage, Charcoal and Other Simple Treatments*, New Lifestyle Books, Seale, AL 36875.

SUPPORT and RESOURCES

B. Nutritional references highly recommended:
1. Scharffenberg, John, MD, *Problems With Meat,* Woodbridge Press, PO Box 6189, Santa Barbara, CA 93111.
2. Thrash, Agatha, MD, and Thrash, Calvin, MD, *Nutrition for Vegetarians,* New Lifestyle Books, Seale, AL 36875.
3. Thrash, Agatha, MD, and Thrash, Calvin, MD, *The Animal Connection,* New Lifestyle Books, Seale, Al 36875.
4. United States Department of Agriculture, *Nutritive Value of Foods,* Superintendent of Documents, U.S. Government Printing Office, Washington, D.C. 20402.
C. Family Health Records: Keep a notebook for your anecdotal records of illnesses and successful procedures, growth records, immunizations, and doctor and hospital visits.
D. Provide for yourself telephone contact with a person whose knowledge of natural remedies and simple treatments you trust. I have been blessed to have had several people fill this role. Dr. Robert and Anne Dunn of Michigan, Doctors Agatha and Calvin Thrash of Uchee Pines Institute, and Lois Dull of Living Springs Retreat. Each have unselfishly given me of their time and medical knowledge, and I am grateful to them.
E. Prayer and consultation with God, the Creator of the human body, Who programmed the body to repair itself.
F. Anatomy and physiology texts:
1. Nilsson, Lennert, *Behold Man: A Photographic Journey Inside the Body,* Little Brown, 1974.
2. Kapi and Wynn, *The Anatomy Coloring Book,* Harper and Row, NY, 1977.
G. Medical encyclopedias and dictionaries.
H. Emergency and first aid references:
1. American Red Cross, *Standard First Aid and Personal Safety,* Doubleday, NY, 1980.
2. American Red Cross, *Life Saving Rescue and Water Safety,* Doubleday, NY, 1977.
I. Self-Care references on specific health problems -Allergy:
1. Austin, Phylis and Thrash, Agatha, MD, *Food Allergies Made Simple,* New Lifestyle Books, Seale, AL 36875.
2. Randolph, Theron, MD, *An Alternative Approach to Allergies.* For further listings, refer to Allergy Reference Bibliography.

J. Health periodicals:
1. *Emphasis Your Health*, Uchee Pines Newsletter, Seale, Al 36875
2. Lifeline Health Letter, Quiet Hour, 630 Brookside Ave., PO Box 3000, Red-lands, CA 92373.
3. *The Journal of Health and Healing,* PO Box 109, Wildwood, GA 30757.
K. Self-care classes and demonstrations:
1. American Red Cross first aid and CPR classes.
2. Uchee Pines Institute - seminars and talks given by Agatha Thrash, MD. 30 Uchee Pines Road, Box 75 Seale AL36875 for information. Phone 205-855-4780.
3. Vegetarian nutrition and cooking classes.
   a. Country Life Restaurants, 112 Broad Street, Boston, MA 02110. Phone: 617-350-8846. Call for affiliates in the United States, Japan, France, and England.
   b. New York City Health Center and Restaurant, an affiliate of Living Springs Retreat, 116 E. 60th St., New York, NY 10022. Call 212-319-7850.
   c. Contact your local Seventh-day Adventist Church for cooking class information given by the churches.
L. Tape services:
1. American Cassette Ministries, P.O. Box 922, Harrisburg, PA 17108.
2. Tel-Med, Box 170, Colton, CA., 100 offices around United States.
3. Weimar Institute Tape Club, Weimar, CA. Phone: 800-824-8916.
4. Wildwood Tape Library, Wildwood, GA 30757.
5. Uchee Pines, 30 Uchee Pines Rd # 1, Seale, AL 36875.
M. Centers of natural healing and health education, located in peaceful, natural settings, provide live-in programs and out-patient consultations. Lifestyle instruction in healthful living, natural remedies, simple treatments, and cholesterol-free cooking is provided, as well as medically supervised physical and health testing. Hydrotherapy, massage, and physical therapy give further support in helping lower blood pressure, manage weight or diabetes, stop smoking, decrease coronary risk factors, and deal with other degenerative diseases, such as arthritis, stress-related problems or allergies.

SUPPORT and RESOURCES

1. Black Hills Health and Education Center, Box 1, Hermosa, SD 57744. Phone: 606-255-4101.
2. Eden Valley Institute, 6263 N. Country Rd., No. 29, Loveland, CO. 80538. Phone: 303-667-6912.
3. Hartland Health Center, PO Box 1, Rapidan, VA 22733. Phone: 703-672-3100.
4. Living Springs Retreat, Bryant Pond Rd., Putnam Valley, NY 10579. Phone: 914-526-2800.
5. Pine Forest Sanitarium and Hospital, Route 1, Box 35, Chunky, MS 39323. Phone: 601-655-8136.
6. Poland Spring Health Institute, RFD#1, Box 4300, Summit Spring Rd. Poland Spring, ME 04274. Phone: 207-998-2894.
7. Newstart Health Center, Weimar Institute, Weimar, CA 95736. Phone: 800-824-8916.
8. Wildwood Sanitarium and Hospital, Wildwood, GA 30757. Phone: 404-820-1493.
9. Uchee Pines Institute, 30 Uchee Pines Rd #1, Seale, AL 36875. Phone: 205-855- 4764.

The Be Prepared Home Medical Kit

Use a carry-on suitcase with inside and outside zip pockets, a large diaper bag, or a heavy cardboard box. Or set aside a section in your bathroom closet to centralize your medical supplies. Make a more compact version for your car or to take with you on vacations or camping trips.

First Aid Supplies:

Emergency Telephone List	Razor blades	Band Aids
Poison Chart	Safety Pins	Gauze Pads
Paper and Pencils	Needle and Thread	Adhesive Tape
Paper Towels	Matches	Ace Bandage
Cotton Balls	Q-tips	

Pharmacy Supplies

Antiseptic	Hydrogen Peroxide
Burns	Aloe Vera gel or plant
Canker Sores	Zinc Gluconate vitamin tablet
Cleanser	Isopropyl alcohol
Indigestion	Charcoal tablets

SUPPORT and RESOURCES

Lubricant .... Vaseline, K-Y Jelly Non-Petroleum
Poison Antidote .... Charcoal
Poison Ivy .... Fel's Naptha Brown Soap,
                                          Ruhlicream
Relaxant .... Catnip tea
Soaking Solution .... Epsom Salts, Baking Soda
Toothaches .... Oil of Cloves
Under-arm Cleanser .... Witch Hazel
Vaporizer Inhalant .... Oil of Eucalyptus

Equipment

Digital Thermometer
Bath Thermometer
Oral Thermometer
Tweezers
Pocket Magnifier
Scissors
Flashlight
Dental Mirror
Ear Syringe or Infant Syringe
Nose Irrigator
Eye Dropper
Eye Wash Cup
Basin for Foot Baths

Hot Water Bottle
Enema Kit
Ice Bag or Zip Loc bags
Heating Compress Materials:
    cotton sheeting
    plastic wrap
    flannel
    safety pins
Heating Pad
Vaporizer
Blood Pressure Cuff
Stethoscope
Otoscope

Mail Order and Source Information

Natural Food Products Mail Order

NAME	PRODUCTS
Garden Spot Distributors (Shiloh Farms) Route 1, Box 729A New Holland, PA 17557	Whole foods Whole buckwheat seeds for sprouting Amaranth seed Non-wheat breads Herbs
Grain Country Food Store 3448-30th Street San Diego, CA 92104 1-619-298-5913	Organic whole foods

SUPPORT and RESOURCES

Green Earth
2545 Praire
Evanston, IL 60201
1-800-322-3662

Organic foods
Caters to the allergic people

Jaffe Brothers, Inc.
P.O. Box 636
Valley Center, CA 92082
1-619-749-1133

National distributors of
   natural foods

Journal Marketing
Box 109
Wildwood, GA 30757
1-615-622-2451

Solait-powdered soy beverage
Dried fruit
Arrowhead Mills products

Mountain Ark Trader
120 South East Ave.
Fayetteville, AR 72701
1-800-643-8900

Macrobiotic foods

Carole Hart
New City Market
1810 N. Halsted St.
Chicago IL 60614
1-312-280-7600

Organic whole foods

**Ozark Cooperative
   Warehouse**
401 Watson Street
P.O. Box 30
Fayetteville. AR 72701
1-501-521-COOP

Catalog and bimonthly
   newsletter/
price list with 900 natural
   food products

Walnut Acres
Penns Creek, PA 17862
717-837-8601

Canned organic vegetables
Full variety of whole foods,
   granolas
Raw buckwheat groats
Corn spaghetti and elbows

SUPPORT and RESOURCES

Grains

Arrowhead Mills
P.O. Box 2059
Hereford, TX 79045
1-800-858-4308

Amaranth, organic grain and
beans
Good source for information

Birkett Mills
P.O. Box 440
Penn Yan, NY 14527
1-315-536-3311

Raw buckwheat
Cream of buckwheat cereal

Grainfields
Weetabix Co.
20 Cameron St.
Clinton, MA 01510
1-800-343-0590

Dry cereal
Rice
Corn

Lundberg Brown Rice
Wehah Farms, Inc.
5370 Church St.
P.O. Box 369
Richvale, CA 95974

Organic rice
Rice cakes
Rice syrup
Rice crunchies

Maskal Injera
318 Willow
Caldwell, ID 83605
1-208-454-3330

Teff - the only cultivated
Bragrotis member of
grass genus

Rodale Press
East Minor St.
Emmaus, PA 18049
Book Department: 1-800-527-8200
Customer Service: 1-800-441-7761

Information on amaranth and
national listings of organic
farmers

Sanctuary Farms
Micheal and Laurie Jones
RD# 1, Butler Rd.
Box 184-A
New London, OH 44851
1-419-929-8177

Certified organic grains,
beans and seeds
Amaranth
Buckwheat

SUPPORT and RESOURCES

Quinoa Corporation
2300 Central Ave.
Boulder, CO 80301
1-800-237-2304

Quinoa: grain, flour and
corn-quinoa pasta

Sea Vegetables

Emes Kosher Jell
19W247-14th Place
Lombard, IL 60148

Vegetable gelatin

Gem Cultures
30301 Sherwood Rd.
Fort Bragg, CA 95437
1-707-964-2922

Tofu coagulants
Sea vegetables

Maine Coast Sea Vegetables
Franklin, ME 04634

Mendocino Sea Vegetables Co.
P.O. Box 372
Navarro, CA 05463
1-707-895-3741

North American Kelp
Cross Street
Waldoboro, ME 04572
1-207-832-7506

Ocean Harvest
P.O. Box 1719
Mendocino, CA 95460
1-707-964-7869

SUPPORT and RESOURCES

Oriental Foods

The Chinese Kitchen
P.O. Box 218
Stirling, NJ 07980

Bean thread noodles
Chinese vermicelli
  rice noodles
Rice paper

Live Food Products
Box 7
Santa Barbara, CA 93102

Bragg's Liquid Aminos-an
  alternative to soy sauce or
tamari

Star Market
3349 N. Clark Street
Chicago, IL 60657
1-312-472-2184

Charcoal

New Lifestyle Books
Seale AL 36875
205 855-4708

Non-dairy Cheese

**Nasheming Valley Natural
   Foods**
Gingko Industrial Park
So. Louise Drive
Iceland, PA 18974

No Moochee
  sesame cheese

American Natural Snacks
P.O. Box 1067
St. Augustine, FL 32084

Soya Kaas
  contains calcium caseinate

Galaxy Cheese Co.
RD#3, Northgate Industrial Park
Box 5204
New Castle, PA 16101
1-800-441-9419

Soymage
(no casein)

Pizsoy
P.O. Box 1314
Cherry Hill, NJ 08003
1-609-354-8036

Uses Soyco, a casein cheese
  made by Galaxy
All natural, no preservatives

SUPPORT and RESOURCES

Vmc Corp.
92 Maple Street
Weehawkeen, NJ 07087

liquid vegetable rennet
derived from mushrooms

Support Groups

Allergy Information Association, 25 Poynter Dr., Room 7, Weston, Ontario M9R 1 K8, Canada - quarterly newsletter.

Allergy Relief Newsletter, Rodale Press Emmaus, PA 18049.

American Allergy Association, P.O. Box 7273, Menlo Park, CA 94025 - bimonthly newsletter.

American Celiac Society, 45 Gifford Ave, Jersey City, NJ 07304.

Asthma and Allergy Foundation of America, 19 W. 44th St., Room 702, New York, NY 10017.

Feingold Associations of the US Drawer A-G, Haltsville, NY 11742.

Human Ecology Action League (H.E.A.L.), 505 N. Lake Shore Dr., Suite 6506, Chicago IL 60611.

Human Ecology Research Foundation of the Southwest, 12110 Webbs Chapel Rd.,Suite 305 E, Dallas, 75234.

Mastering Food Allergies - (newsletter) Mast Enterprises Inc., 1500 N. Wilmot Rd., Deerfield IL 60015.

INDEX

INDEX

OTHER FINE BOOKS AVAILABLE FROM FAMILY HEALTH PUBLICATIONS

VEGETARIAN COOKBOOKS

TASTE AND SEE: ALLERGY RELIEF COOKING / Penny King	11.95
OF THESE YE MAY FREELY EAT / Jo Ann Rachor	2.95
OF THESE YE MAY FREELY EAT SUPPLEMENT: **PRACTICAL INSTRUCTION IN COOKING AND NUTRITION** Jo Ann Rachor	2.95
THE COUNTRY LIFE VEGETARIAN COOKBOOK	9.95
RECIPES FROM THE WEIMAR KITCHEN / Weimar Institute	9.95
THE JOY OF COOKING NATURALLY / Peggy Dameron	9.95
COOKING WITH NATURAL FOODS / Muriel Beltz	14.95
COOKING WITH NATURAL FOODS II / Muriel Beltz	14.95
EAT FOR STRENGTH / Agatha Thrash, M.D.	7.95
EAT FOR STRENGTH (Oil Free Edition) / Agatha Thrash, M.D.	7.95
COUNTRY KITCHEN COLLECTION / Silver Hills Institute	11.95
TEN TALENTS / Hurd	16.95
100% VEGETARIAN: EATING NATURALLY FROM YOUR **GROCERY STORE** / Julianne Pickle	5.95
STRICT VEGETARIAN COOKBOOK / Lorine Tadej	7.95

NATURAL REMEDIES, LIFESTYLE, NUTRITION ETC.

NUTRITION FOR VEGETARIANS / Agatha & Calvin Thrash, M.D.	9.95
HOME REMEDIES / Agatha & Calvin Thrash, M.D.	9.95
NATURAL REMEDIES / Austin, Thrash & Thrash, M.D.	6.95
MORE NATURAL REMEDIES / Austin, Thrash & Thrash, M.D.	6.95
FOOD ALLERGIES MADE SIMPLE / Austin, Thrash & Thrash, M.D.	4.95
PRESCRIPTION: CHARCOAL / Agatha & Calvin Thrash, M.D.	6.95
FATIGUE: CAUSES, TREATMENT AND PREVENTION / Austin, Thrash & Thrash, M.D.	4.95
ANIMAL CONNECTION / Agatha & Calvin Thrash, M.D.	4.95
PMS: PREMENSTRUAL SYNDROME / Agatha & Calvin Thrash, M.D.	2.95
NEW START / Vernon Foster, M.D.	9.95
HOME MADE HEALTH / Raymond & Dorothy Moore	11.95
GARLIC FOR HEALTH / Dr. Benjamin Lau	3.95
NATURAL HEALTHCARE FOR YOUR CHILD / Austin, Thrash & Thrash	9.95
HYDROTHERAPY: / Clarence Dail M.D., Charles Thomas Ph. D.	8.95
CASE AGAINST COFFEE AND OTHER BROWN DRINKS / Agatha & Calvin Thrash, M.D.	2.50

Order From:

Family Health Publications
8777 E. Musgrove Hwy.
Sunfield, MI 48890

Subtotal _____
Mi Residents
(4% Sales Tax) _____

Shipping:
$2.00 First Book
.50 Each Addl. _____

Total Amt. Encl._____